THE COACH

PATRICK MOURATOGLOU

WYMER
PUBLISHING
Bedford, England

First published in Great Britain in 2017
by Wymer Publishing
www.wymerpublishing.co.uk
Tel: 01234 326691
Wymer Publishing is a trading name of Wymer (UK) Ltd

ISBN 978-1-908724-75-5 (paperback)
ISBN 978-1-908724-76-2 (eBook)

Translation by Paul Newman.
Edited by Joel R. Byrom.

Typeset by Wymer.
Printed and bound in England by
Clays, Bungay, Suffolk.

A catalogue record for this book is available from the British Library.

Design by Wymer.
Cover images © Antoine Couvercelle
For TV appearances Patrick Mouratoglou is represented by:
Michael P. Cohen, MPC Entertainment
Website: www.mpce.com | Email: mpce@mpce.com
For all other business please contact Patrick Mouratoglou at: patrick@mouratoglou.com.

THE COACH

PATRICK MOURATOGLOU

" *Whenever you do anything, be aware that you will be opposed by those who wanted to do the same thing, by those who wanted to do the opposite and by the vast majority of those who wanted to do nothing.* "

Confucius

Without my parents,
I would have been someone else.

Without my three children,
I would be lacking a central pillar of my life.

Without those who were bold enough to believe
in me, I would not have been able to achieve
anything.

Without those who opposed me,
I would never have learned how to fight.

Without those who gave me love,
I would never have existed.

A Coach

*When you embark on the adventure you need ambition
but also freedom from any cares;*

*Humility as you set out on each new collaboration,
because when you begin working with someone you
need to start with a clean slate;*

*A healthy dose of self-assurance to enable you to
impose yourself on the person you are working with;*

*Love and empathy,
so that you can be an attentive and kind listener;*

*An acute sense of observation and analysis to
determine precisely what your student needs, as well as
intuition, so that you can anticipate what he is feeling
without him having to tell you;*

*The passion to live intensely through events and to
keep faith, as well as enough detachment to enable you
to be objective in any situation;*

*The desire to put into work a plan of action and the
discipline to stick to it, as well as perseverance and
optimism to keep heading in the right direction, even
when a storm is raging around you;*

The rigour to map out a strategy;

The creativity to negotiate a route off the beaten track;

Patience to accept the length of the road, and impatience to impose on yourself the constant need to move forward;

A sense of communication so that you are in sync with your student and diplomacy to make your whole team stick together;

Experience so that you can avoid foundering on the rocks;

Huge confidence in yourself so that you can convey the necessary strength to bring a project, however insane it might seem, to a successful conclusion.

That's what being a coach is.

Contents

Contents

Foreword

It was the summer of 2012. I had just won Miami, Charleston, Madrid and reached the semis of Rome but had to pull out to make sure I was in full form, fully fit and fully ready for the main event: The only Grand Slam that eluded me for ten years, Roland-Garros. I won it once before, ten years prior, but it seemed like, no matter what I did or did not do, I managed to loose at Roland-Garros every year. Now at thirty and on paper for tennis, "over the hill" I wanted to try to do something new: Win Roland-Garros.

Before the tournament started I would often see Patrick Mouratoglou. A coach that always intrigued me because he was always able to bring people to a new level. I remember playing his student Aravane Rezai in Sydney, Australia one year and wow I was in trouble. I had to fight deep to win that match. She went on to nearly break the top ten under his tutelage. There was also Wickmayer who managed to get to the semis of the U.S. Open almost instantly with his help.

Patrick was fearless, he was nice and he seemed to always be around. I always bumped into him everywhere I went at RG 2012. Even before my first round match I saw him and I told him, "as always I have to play a local French woman in the first round. It seems like every year I have to play someone French!"

Then, I crashed out first round at Court Philippe–Chatrier. I was devastated. I spent three days in my room. I never left. I just stayed in, wondering what next. I did everything I needed to do to win, but mentally I fell apart. I came undone. I'm not sure why, but I just could not get it together.

After also loosing in the first round of the doubles, I decided either to go home or go to work. Home was not appealing. I loved France. I loved the culture, I had a small apartment there and I wanted to work. But how? It hit me: coach Mouratoglou.

After getting in contact with him he proposed I went to his academy and hit ball with two guys every day. The first day, the Coach did not seem as fiery and fearless as he normally does. He was docile, sensitive and open. He came on to the court with me and I thought wow, well why doesn't he stay and tell me some things? I want to see how this coach manages to make people turn corners they normally don't. That first day, I will never forget, because I don't remember him saying a single word. I turned around and said, "if you want to interject feel free. I am just here to learn and I am completely open to hear new things."

Until that moment in my thirteen Grand Slam career I had always worked with my dad and my mum. But I was not looking for anything else I was just looking to win.

I don't remember what happened and what Patrick said, but I do remember loving it. He sounded just like my dad! Confident in me, fearless and hungry. He loved how I used open stances and encouraged me to continue using them. I often had people tell me that I should NOT use that footwork and they were quickly out. It was the same coaching style, innovative and confident.

When it came time for me to go I did not want to stop working and listening to him. I tasted something new and fresh and I wanted to keep it up. I asked him if maybe he could work with me at Wimbledon before the tournament because I knew he was working with someone else at the time. He said he would have to talk to his student and get back with me. Again his honesty, I thought, was great.

I was so excited. I talked with my mum and told her working with Mouratoglou was cool. He worked like I wanted to. I wanted to take my game to a new level and even though I was thirty I knew I could do it. She was excited for me. So a week before Wimbledon, I worked everyday with Patrick and my dad.

But I struggled. I was winning my matches but barely. My confidence was a bit lower than normal. I was sick, I just was not myself. Finally I somehow managed to get into the quarter–finals in both singles and doubles and Patrick was talking to me before my match. He told me, "Up until now I have seen a mediocre Serena. I want to see the real Serena, the one that is great. You have not brought her out yet. I've seen her on television, but today is the day she needs to come out. Without her you will not win."

He was right I was really passive all week and I was going up against the defending champion, I needed something extra.

So Serena came out and he has helped me bring "Serena" out ever since. I went on to win singles and doubles that year at Wimbledon; Singles at the U.S. Open and the end of the year championships. Soon I was back at number one. I was now apart of Patrick Mouratoglou's tutelage, that winning one.

Patrick Mouratoglou is the "Mastermind" indeed. I wanted something fresh, something different, something that was able to take me from great to historic. That is what Patrick was able to do with me. In just two years we went to win six out of eleven Grand Slams ALL FOUR OF THEM and countless other titles including the year end championships three times in a row and lead me to my dream of holding an Olympic Gold Medal. Patrick analyses situations, and conforms them to fit whoever he works with, professional tennis players, amateurs, juniors, or just for motivation. He takes the confidence that is in him and it somehow permeates into you.

Patrick is not a great coach but a phenomenal coach. The only thing is, you haven't seen the best of him yet. He is still working on his masterpiece and for anyone facing whoever he is coaching – that is a fearful thought.

Serena Williams

1
Running out of inspiration

"I believe in the sun, even when it is not shining."
Graffiti by a Holocaust victim

Unbelievable... I have been feeling tired for some months now – yet I'm someone who has always been brimming over with energy. I feel less inspired, less alert, less creative. Everything seems to me to be insurmountable – yet I'm someone who has always tackled life with a ferocious enthusiasm.

This weariness has been dragging me down for months, but at last I have come to understand what is going on inside me, what has made me grind to a halt, what has stopped me in my tracks.

I have come a long way – a very long way. In truth, I have come from nowhere. My life had been set out for me, yet I had no desire to embark on a journey that had been prepared for me in advance. Then I started up an engine – an internal engine with phenomenal power.

I put my dreams into words and I decided to

make them happen: mad dreams, sub–conscious dreams, which all my friends and those close to me said were impossible to achieve. People said I was a dreamer, a gentle eccentric setting out to scale an unclimbable Everest.

Twenty years later I'm standing on the terrace of my academy and reality hits me straight in the face. I have achieved every one of my ambitions. Better than that, beyond all my hopes I have actually exceeded them.

Obviously, life does not end there. Obviously, I have thousands of things still to accomplish, even though this once sickly child, who lacked confidence but dreamed about tennis when watching television, has become a big player on this particular stage. I am the coach of one of the greatest women players of all time, who under my guidance has returned to number one in the world and enjoyed the best seasons of her career despite being over 30 years old. I am the founder and president of one of the world's biggest tennis academies. I am a consultant and commentator for Eurosport International, and my show *The Coach* is broadcasted daily in more than 50 countries during Grand Slams, a published author and a consultant for several tennis magazines across the world...

I started my foundation named *Champ'Seed* to help the best hopes in tennis who need financial support achieve their dreams.

I started a family and have three wonderful

children.

When I assess my life I ask myself: what is driving me forward today? I would like to catch a glimpse of at least the start of a reply to that question, but the engine has seized up. It's like I have a hangover. I had been moving forward like a steamroller: when I decided on something, when I wanted something, nothing got in my way. I just pushed ahead, broke down the doors – and got in through the windows if necessary. When people tried to stop me I just carried on regardless. I had dedicated my professional life to finding ways to get what I wanted for my players and for myself.

But as I write those words, I can't express what it is that drives me on. Recognition? I've enjoyed that beyond my wildest dreams.

Meeting people? I've been able to approach most of those people who inspired me. I can confirm with gratitude that no door is closed to me. Money? I earn a very good living, but that has never been motivation for me.

Titles? We have won more than I could have dared to dream about winning. I count them in tens, including eight Grand Slam titles and two Olympic gold medals.

What then? Absolutely nothing.

I have achieved everything that had seemed out of my reach, thanks to my total dedication, a huge amount of work and remaining focused throughout.

I have dreamed, planned, suffered, fought and had sleepless nights. I have made every sacrifice in order to achieve my goals. Today everything is possible to me, everything is within my reach. All I have left to do is to harvest the fruits of my years of work. But I know that this feeling is an illusion. I know equally that if I relax I could lose everything in the space of one second.

In writing these words I am well aware that my own existential problems might seem futile and unimportant. However, I am going through a period of depression and have only just woken up to that fact.

I need excitement. I need mad dreams which tear me away from my comfort zone. I always want to stand up to, challenge, frighten myself.

That is what drives me. In reaching all my objectives, I have lost what is most precious to me, what drove me forward, what made me fight.

I've always wanted to strive for excellence, to lead a fulfilled life, to leave a mark. A life is so fleeting... I would like mine to be a collection of exceptional moments. It's a race against the clock because there are so many things to achieve and yet so little time. I've always thought that I could achieve everything, all that I had dreamed about and everything that I will dream about tomorrow. However, this frenzy that had always carried me forward has just left me.

When the French editor suggested that I should

write an autobiography my first reaction was: "I'm in my forties. At this moment in time that doesn't make any sense. Let's talk about it again when I'm 80."

She then explained to me that it was precisely my exceptional life journey that made for such a gripping subject: the success story of an outsider, a man with no advantages.

As I write these words, after Serena, coached by me, has just enjoyed the best seasons of her career, I realise that my strength, what makes me special, is my ability to resolve whole sets of problems, my ability to bounce back.

I recall where I came from and I feel as if I have been saved by a miracle.

Me, the sickly child.

Me, the boy who was an academic failure.

Me, the adolescent who was so reserved that he could not communicate with people.

This career on which I had embarked was not pre–destined.

How had this puny boy, uncomfortable in his own skin, become a leader of men and women?

How had I managed to conquer my timidity and my complexes to transform myself into a communicator who was able to enter the world of my players?

How had I broken free from the spiral of failure to become someone who turned others into winners?

How had I been able to change a tale which had started out so unpromisingly into a success story?

Life often turns on a few major decisions, which you take at crucial moments. The same is true of a player's career. When you make those decisions, you have to trust that your will does not fail you.

As far as I am concerned, four major decisions have allowed me to make radical turns on my life path, to reinvent myself and to adapt in order to get what I expected out of life. I had set out on a life of mediocrity, but I fought to change my destiny. I was unwell but I recovered my health. I was indecisive and I learned to lead my life the way I wanted to. I was fearful but I have become fearless.

Everything is possible. Nothing is set in stone. Life is a tennis match. You set out with potential, with a dream, with fears and with uncertainties. With faith, ambition, courage, perseverance – and with a lack of awareness – you can move mountains.

Here is my life, my match, my journey.

2
My Wimbledon

*"Take your opportunity, grab your good fortune
and take on your risk.
They will get used to looking at you."*

René Char

July 8th 2012
Wimbledon, London, United Kingdom

Serena is facing Agnieszka Radwanska, the
world No.2, in the Wimbledon final. It's a
chance for her to win a Grand Slam title, which she
hasn't done for two years. We have been working
together for a month. She is playing for high stakes.
She has taken a risk by deciding to choose me. It's
the first time in her career that she has gone to a
private coach, having only ever worked with her
father. She wants to get back to the top and this is
the first Everest she has to climb. The crisis of
confidence that she has been through has pushed

her to leave her comfort zone, to change her ways, to go back to the drawing board.

For me too this match is crucial in many respects. It is an opportunity to prove how well our partnership is working; on the other hand it could call that partnership into question. It could enable me to win my first Grand Slam title as a coach, which had been my goal ever since I decided to become a professional tennis coach.

The early rounds have been very difficult, but I could also point out that the results of our work together have become apparent with each match. I am getting to know my player better and better and my contributions are having more and more impact. I can sense her mental state and I can influence it to the extent that she goes into matches in the best possible frame of mind. She gets nearer to her best level as she advances in the tournament. When Serena is in the zone she is untouchable.

When the match is interrupted by rain at one set all and she gives me a look which says she wants to see me outside the locker rooms, I know that I will find the words that will make a difference. I also know that when she looks me in the eyes during this short conversation she will discover the reassurance and the confidence she needs in order to go back into battle even stronger.

"When you win, don't say anything. When you lose, say even less."

Paul Brown

Twenty–seven minutes later, a victorious Serena shakes Radwanska's hand. She has won. We have won.

I am happy, but only because her joy is so clear to me. I take pride in a job accomplished, having played a decisive role. That's it. Nothing else. It's as though everything had been written in the stars, as if I had arrived at that point just as I had always expected to. No surprise, no luck. Step by step I have followed the route which took me to this final. It was a path which had become clear beneath my feet, little by little, over more than fifteen years. Even if there had been moments when I had strayed from that path, I always knew that I would reach my destination. My path was a reflection of this tournament that Serena had toiled so hard to win.

At the end of the match I don't feel any desire to explode with joy. I want to go home. My mission has been accomplished and I am exhausted. I don't hang around inside the stadium. I am walking towards my rented apartment when my phone rings. It's Serena: "Where are you? What are you doing? This is a time when you should be with us. Come straight away." She is extremely excited, as if she had just won the first Grand Slam title of her career.

For me, it's all very different. I have finally realised this dream of helping a player to win a Grand Slam title. I have finally achieved this goal that I had set myself as a coach. I had achieved all my other goals one after another, but this has been the fruit of my whole career. I hadn't won my Grand Slam that day. I had won it stage by stage, day after day.

Just after the match a throng of journalists gather round me with cameras, voice recorders and microphones in hand. The questions come thick and fast about Serena, about what to make of her revival, about our work together. When one of the journalists asks if working with her is like a consecration for me, I retort: "No. That's not the situation. I don't look on my work like that. I'll only be satisfied if I am really able to make the difference. Serena is a great champion with or without me. My job is to help her reach another dimension, to make her win more than she has ever done before, to break records. That is the only way in which I will be able to judge the quality of my work."

The tournament is over and I know that from now onwards, beginning from tomorrow, I will refocus on new objectives. The season continues and the Olympic Games take place in only three weeks' time.

What happened today is not the end of a story, this is not a conclusion. This is the start of a new and incredible adventure: my adventure, which I have been building for fifteen years – our adventure, which we embarked upon just a month ago. I don't know what the future will bring, but at this moment I am convinced that we have an appointment with tennis history.

3

A chaotic childhood

"In the depths of winter I finally learned that within me there lay an invincible summer."
Albert Camus

I have come a long way. The road has been so long that I have trouble appreciating the length of the journey. I have trouble understanding how the child that I was, could have become the adult who is writing these words today. Much of that is down to tennis, but what has always made the difference has been my refusal to accept fate, my obsession with grabbing hold of life and moulding it to my dreams, my ability to evolve into the person that I want to be. I have achieved this tour de force through my unshakeable will and my great capacity to adapt. I have learned to develop these qualities – and I regard them as my greatest professional assets. I have changed my destiny, though I needed many years to do that...

As a child, my life was full of suffering. Every

day I endured anxiety attacks at night. I suffered with nausea and vomiting. I was puny and very timid. I felt like someone who was looking in disbelief at my own life, paralysed by the shame of not being able to do better.

I judged myself without any kindness. I admired others for their qualities – and I didn't find any in myself. I was very reserved. Even in the best situations I needed a lot of time to form friendships with other people. Added to that, I was frustratingly slow to grow physically, to the point where I was always the smallest in my class. I lived in a hermetically sealed bubble and even the most minimal of contact with other people required exhausting effort.

On top of everything, I had some serious difficulties at school. School crystallised all my problems. I spent most of my time there alone, unhappy and in a state of failure. My father kept me under permanent pressure. He had always been a brilliant student and blamed my failure at school on a lack of desire on my part. He was not around often because he was always working and travelled a lot. Even when he was there in the family home, his spirit was elsewhere. His head was always in his business. He got up early in the morning, played classical piano for two hours and then left for the office. He came home for dinner, got down from the table as soon as he had eaten his last mouthful and worked until he went to bed.

When my brother or I talked to him, he did not give us his full attention and replied in vague terms. He was absorbed instead by his professional projects and by his clever calculations.

My father was born in Greece to Greek parents. He left the country of his birth when he was thirteen. Having been a brilliant student, he then pursued a remarkable professional career.

At 16 he gave up studying for his baccalaureate and entered the *Ecole Polytechnique* after only one year at preparatory school.

A lover of classical music, as his parents were, he played the piano for several hours each day, as he still does to this day. It was as if my childhood was spent being rocked to sleep as he practised his scales. I write these pages to the sound of Chopin's nocturnes: musical works of great purity, muffled and intimate, which remind me of my childhood, my family, my roots. They fill me with nostalgia.

While preparing to enter the *Polytechnique*, my father recorded an album of him playing classical piano. He briefly considered giving up his studies for a career as a soloist. The choice he made at that moment was crucial in terms of the rest of his professional life. His future success in the world of business would tell him that he made the right decision.

Nonetheless, I doubt whether social success has ever been an objective for him. He regards business as an art. He tells me: "A good bit of business is a masterpiece." Everything is perfectly conceived, implemented and thought–through and eventually fits together as if by magic. He is not materialistic. He could afford to indulge every material fancy he might ever have, but he drives an old saloon car, which has seen better days. Totally unmoved by the jibes of his two sons, he has never changed.

My father is a business intellectual, gifted with great pragmatism. He started out with his own father, a Greek immigrant who arrived in France without any money, having lost everything in the war. They went into property development and my father quickly took charge. He made a name for himself with some prestigious projects, like the port of Deauville and all its marinas; the port of Saint–Raphael and the Annonciade tower block in Monaco, which is the biggest in the whole of the principality.

Then one bad business deal saw him lose most of his money. He had to start again from nothing and even had to sell his car, though he was soon back on an even keel.

A few years earlier he had become one of the pioneers of renewable energy. At that time technological developments like solar panels and wind turbines did not produce enough energy to produce a return on investment. He had the idea of using fiscal legislation in place at the time to offer tax benefits, which would be compensation for the low returns. He was one of the first people in

France to set up major businesses in this area. He created two companies, one in France and the other in the United States, with a business partner who was prepared to go and live abroad. Some years later the American subsidiary became the biggest privately–owned American company in the energy sector. It went on the New York stock exchange. The same happened with the French subsidiary. Quoted on the stock exchange, it attracted capital investment from EDF and became the latter's specialist subsidiary in renewable energy. My father ran the company for many years and then sold his shares to the nationalised company in 2011.

At the age of 70 he created a new company, called *EREN*. He continued to invest in renewable energy by buying start–up companies which were developing innovative new technologies in this field.

Throughout my youth, about once a month, he would sit me down face to face and set about giving me what I regarded at the time as a moral lesson about my chaotic school life. We were worlds apart. He did not try to understand what I was feeling, or most probably he was unable to. Instead he just tried to hammer into me the importance of my studies. Then he would disappear, leaving me to face insoluble problems on my own. What would go without saying on his part appeared to me to be even more insurmountable. I did not have a clue and was simply left to fend for myself. He was certainly prepared to spend an hour or two helping me to resolve a particular mathematical problem, but he didn't know how to teach me to become a better student. I was at a real dead–end. I could not see a way out because my failure at school, combined with the pressures I felt on my shoulders, created an emotional situation that I just could not control.

Sitting at my desk for hours on end every evening as I tried to do my homework, my life was real agony. I did not understand anything, I did not remember anything from what I learnt. I felt sick and wanted to scream. I dreamed of the day when I would finally be free from my studies, but that seemed so far away! My ill–being grew with every day that passed.

Going to high school fellow schoolchildren went for me and spat in my face, taking advantage of my weakness of character. I stood stock still and did not react. I was incredibly angry with myself. I went back home crying tears of anger. I was afraid. I felt defenceless, belittled and vulnerable. This world did not take pity on the weak. I walked round in a dream in which I would go back to them and give them a good hiding. It was an excellent lesson, which was to give me the means to ensure that I would never be humiliated like that again.

Those years were the worst of my life. I felt weak, unable to react, alone. But it was at that time, when I was a victim of my own weaknesses, that I developed some of the characteristics that would enable me to become the man and the professional that I am today.

Because I just did not have any connection with other people, I was never someone who took part in anything; instead I was always observing my classmates and their relationships with each other. I wanted to know how they went about leading their social lives in a way that I could only dream about. Despite myself, I set about becoming a student of sociology. I listened, I observed, I cross–checked. Outwardly my life might have appeared ghostly, but my inner self was blossoming, fed by my constant observations of what I saw around me.

I observed my classmates and took heed of every detail, every intonation in a voice, every raised eyebrow. With an eye for the tiniest detail, I studied the bonds which connected them. I understood who held power over whom and why. By scrutinising their features and by noting even the smallest details about how they looked each day, I came to feel what they themselves were feeling. I knew when they were proud, when they were upset, when they were shocked, confident, impressed, frightened etc.

The body, the face and the intonation of the voice tell you so much about someone's personality and what they are feeling inside. Little by little, I began to read those signs among my classmates with great precision. I could often guess their reactions when they faced certain situations. I knew them better than anybody – not because I liked them, but precisely because I had no relationship whatsoever with them.

I was never one to take part in anything, which meant that I could always simply observe. I also became aware of the fact that I would know how to speak to them, what words and what tone of voice to use, in order to generate any number of emotions in them. I was becoming a coach without realising it. However, I would always be wary of intervening. Even if, deep down inside me, that was what I secretly dreamed of doing, my unhealthy shyness would not allow it.

I started playing tennis when I was about four. My parents did not set out to make me a champion (to my great despair). They simply took great pleasure in playing tennis because it was a sport that was really taking off in the mid–1970s. They spent their entire weekends at the club and it was quite natural for my brother and I to get together there with a group of children of our own age. As everyone was playing I also had a go – and it was love at first sight. I spent most of my weekends on the court. I was inexhaustible, unlike my practice partners, who had to play against me in relay. I would spend whole days hitting balls. Tennis was where I found my freedom. It was the only place where I felt I was respected, the only place where I could be myself. My shyness disappeared. I felt comfortable with people. At last I was alive. The court was my playground, my kingdom.

Now I look back on myself when I was 25. At that time I was working alongside my father in his company. I had stopped playing tennis, but I used to go and have lunch regularly at a tennis club, alongside the courts. I let my imagination wander and I saw so many things. Above all I saw a geometric pattern, a theatre of infinite possibilities.

Tennis is maths. If you understand the simply geometry involved, you can acquire a very good tactical understanding of the sport.

Tennis is also about emotion: the emotion that I felt when I thought about those courts, which brought back all the feelings that I used to know. It was my *madeleine*, it was the song that brought back my childhood memories.

Tennis is also about imagination and creativity. With my eyes glued to the court, I created imaginary patterns of play, sometimes for more than an hour.

Without realising it, I was preparing for the third phase of my life. Having been a player and then a businessman in my father's company, I was now to become a tennis coach.

When I was a child my parents did not for one moment think of pointing me in the direction of a sporting career, simply because they had no idea what top-level sport was like. They came from a more traditional environment and an academic upbringing.

I developed my dream in secret. I was working at it; I did not say anything about it, but I was preparing myself.

When I was between the ages of seven and twelve, Roland–Garros was the only televised tennis event, the only tournament which attracted much media coverage in France. Every year I used to count the days until the start of this great moment, like other children might count the days until Christmas. When the tournament started I would stay indoors and gorge myself on the feast of matches. Then I would head out into the garden and play with a plastic racket and a rubber ball against a wall for hours on end. I would play imaginary matches. I created scenarios and lived my imaginary contests as if they were real. This was a great era of tennis, the age of Borg and McEnroe. Paradoxically I was a fan of the Swede, despite the fact that I was an attacking player at heart, an exponent of serve–and–volley and chip–and–charge. I admired his calmness and his charisma. He seemed impervious to pressure and to emotions. In contrast to the American, who was a specialist at blowing his fuse, Borg seemed unshakeable.

> *"The body's sickness is the soul's cure."*
> Basque Proverb

Compared to my father, I felt small and worthless. That reduced me to despair. I was a child beset by problems which I could not resolve. My nightly anxiety attacks and my fragile health were eating away at my life. I didn't sleep at night. I saw imaginary insects everywhere in my bed. I lived in a state of terror. I dreaded bed–time. My mother, who could not have been more dutiful, spent hours at my bedside every night trying in vain to bring me peace.

I was extremely anxious and ultra–sensitive. When I was troubled by any sort of everyday issue, it was always my stomach that would flinch. I would spend the night vomiting, on occasions up to ten times. The memory of those exhausting nights still haunts me today.

When I was thirteen I decided that these problems just had to stop. Against all expectations, the result was immediate. Having spent an umpteenth night of hell vomiting, I just said to myself that it would not happen again. As of that day I have never experienced the same troubles again; and as I write this I am 44 years old. It was my first great victory over myself. It was essential in two respects: above all because it allowed me to break this daily cycle of failure, but also because it made me realise that I had power within me. Considering the sort of child that I was, it was a huge triumph. I could control this body which had caused me so much suffering. I had brought it crashing down. I had beaten it. I had real power over it. It was a crucial discovery. From now on, I would be able to take control of my body and then go on to deal with my other problems.

The nightly anxiety attacks also stopped. Whereas before I had felt burned out and just wanted to fade away, so that my body would stop tormenting me, I had rapidly become aware of the vital power that was lying dormant in me.

This spark, this detonator brought me out of my torpor. At last I would be alive and able to take up the place that belonged to me.

Although I was still prone to a sickly shyness, I started to use this new–found confidence to make friendships. However, it wasn't easy, because on top of my difficulties in reaching out to people, I was out of sync with them. I lived in Neuilly in a upper–class neighbourhood. My parents, in wanting to imbue me with their values, refused to let me follow the dress "codes" that were in vogue at school. I was surrounded by kids wearing *Weston* shoes while I looked like a drop–out. I made friends with other exiles like myself – sons of Jewish "pieds–noirs", Armenians, Lebanese. Our Mediterranean roots brought us together. Looking back, I am grateful to my parents for making those choices. The friendships that I built at that time were very solid. The friends that I made then are still my friends today and I will love them until the day I die. They were the ones who believed in me when I was at my lowest point. That is something that I have not forgotten. Their friendship broke through my deep loneliness. Without knowing it, they saved my life.

"Be yourself. Everyone else is already taken."
Oscar Wilde

Some years later, when I was 15 and had totally taken control of my body, it was time for me to take control of my life. An incident occurred at that time which was to dictate how I would lead the rest of my life.

Having reached 10th grade, my studies occupied more and more of my time, but I needed to go to another level with my tennis. I wanted to practise more and travel in order to take part in international tournaments. I talked to my parents to try and agree on a way forward. At that time my progress had created some interest in the regional league. I practised there three evenings a week and played with people from the club every weekend. I was becoming stronger and stronger, despite one enormous disadvantage: I was slow to grow. I still had the body of a child. I was small and weak. When you're playing serve–and–volley, that's not ideal. I was not a big presence at the net, so I compensated with my physical explosiveness and sense of anticipation. When I was volleying I attracted the ball like a magnet. I read my opponent's passing shots as soon as they were struck and threw myself at the ball.

My parents' response was definitive: there would be no adjustment to my schooling. I would have to see my studies through to the end. Once I had earned my diploma in business or engineering I would be free to play tennis if that was what I wanted. How little they knew about tennis at the highest level! I was stunned. Being a professional tennis player is a race against time. At thirty your career is over in most cases. My parents' refusal sounded the death knell for my professional hopes. I tried in vain to explain to them. It was impossible to get them to listen to reason. As far as my parents were concerned there were two options: one was an ultra high–risk step into a world they did not know and the other amounted to real life insurance. Higher studies had opened doors for my father and had put him on the road to professional success. My parents' culture was intellectual and artistic: literature, classical music, painting. Sport for them was just a hobby.

I felt destroyed. What made me happy, what made me want to get up in the morning, my lifeline, my oxygen – everything had disappeared in just a few minutes. My dream had been taken away from me. I could not believe it.

My dejection was quickly replaced by frustration. I became aggressive and hateful. How could my parents do this to me? Why did they not try to understand me? Why were they refusing to give me this opportunity?

I have never been able to do things by halves. I probably never will, and so much the better. That's my personality. I do everything one hundred per cent, or I do nothing. Since I would be unable to throw myself completely into my tennis, I would give up. I would put my racket in the cupboard. I would turn a new page.

> *"Before becoming a wise old man*
> *you often need to have been a young idiot."*
> Oprah Winfrey

The first year after I gave up tennis was very difficult. I was an adolescent, but I was still introverted and uncomfortable in my own skin. I learned to make use of my hatred and frustration to find the strength to surpass myself and to get my life under way. Stopping tennis left a gaping hole in my young life. I had never previously felt the need to build a social life. I took to dreaming of being a strong adolescent, confident, surrounded by friends, popular at school... all those things that until that moment, had been denied to me.

I had never been one to go out in the evenings. I led an ordered life. Now I would follow all my whims and fancies. I no longer owed anything to parents who were unable to understand or even listen to me. I would become uncontrollable. I had, after all, been able to take control of my body; now it was time to take control of my life. It was at that moment that I found within myself the courage to break with the past.

It was 9.30pm and we had just finished our family evening meal. I had planned to join my friends at a party. My father was an authoritarian figure whose decisions were never challenged. The house rules were strict and I was not allowed to go out in the evenings. All four of us were sitting in the living room. I turned to my parents and I said: "I'm going out this evening."

My father's reply was instant: "No, I don't think so."

"You see the front door of the house at the end of the corridor? I'm going to get up from this sofa, I'm going to walk towards that door, I'm going to open it and I'm going to go out. If you want to prevent me doing that, then that's up to you, but if I were you I wouldn't do it."

There was a heavy silence. I got up and I went out. My father did not move.

From that day onwards I took control of the house. That piece of bravado, for which I nevertheless paid a price, made a new young man out of me. I became aware that I was a decision–maker, that I did actually have a strong personality. I think my parents suddenly realised that too. From that evening onwards, our life was turned on its head. Throughout that time my mother felt it as a blow. She could not understand the ude of this dear son to whom she had given so much. She felt she had lost me. I completely forgot the sacrifices she had made. I had taken a backhand swipe against everything she had given me, against her unrelenting support throughout all those years when I had needed her so much. Even in taking the decision not to go along with my tennis plans she had done so in the certainty that she was acting in my best interests.

Looking back, my behaviour ought to disgust me. I should conclude that I was an ungrateful little devil. But I would hesitate to judge the boy that I was at that time, because life has taught me to beware of making judgements. In my job as a coach, I have learned to make a distinction between people's personalities and their behaviour. I just think that the attitude that I had adopted at that precise moment in time – even if you could take the moral high ground and criticise it – was necessary. It was vital. It was character–forming.

In my job I often come across people who judge others by their behaviour. So–and–so conducts himself in such a way, so he is therefore an egotist, a worrier, a nervous person, a pretentious person etc. Those conclusions are clearly wrong, even if it's reassuring to put labels on people.

Behaviour does not define people. Behaviour is just the response they find most appropriate in a given situation. They might prefer to act differently, but don't know how to go about it.

My job as a coach does not allow me to make judgements. That would be out of place. The first question that I ask myself when I see a player developing is: "Is he or she behaving in a way that will help his or her progress, that will help him or her to win?" Certain behaviour which might seem inappropriate, can be explained in other ways. People adapt their behaviour, in response to different situations, by drawing on the resources at their disposal. From the point of view of a player's progression, if they are not reacting as they should then their behaviour will have to be re–assessed and thereafter modified.

Therefore rather than judge the young rebel that I was, I prefer to ask myself what caused him to act in such a way. I'm not particularly proud of how I behaved, but it was part of my past. Not everything that I did was great but I didn't stop trying to break free from the ball and chain around my neck – sometimes by trampling over people I loved, simply because I didn't know any other way of going about it.

At the time I thought that the break between myself and my parents was definitive. I didn't owe them anything any more and from that moment onwards my life was totally my own. The hatred which rumbled secretly inside me and which I had kept there for so many years was going to come out. I had become a rebel, an aggressor. At school I clashed with the teachers. I talked back to them, I confronted them. I was expelled by several educational establishments. People tried to reason with me, but I was in a world of my own. I went out every evening and I developed a taste for violence. From that moment onwards nobody could make an impression on me. I even started fights myself. I came home late at night, sometimes with my clothes torn and my face swollen. My father was unable to sleep. He was worried about me. He would wait for me to come back, taking up his post in the living room. When I came in through the door I would go straight to my bedroom without saying a word. He would feel relieved and could at last go to bed.

I became a little gang leader, surrounded by bad people. I was hanging around with dealers, little yobs, who were often armed. We drove up and down the streets on scooters and gatecrashed parties.

I was a star. The girls liked me and I took advantage of that. I did that a lot – too much. Alcohol, up all night, cigarettes, violence and sex. The whole lot.

Having been thrown out of three educational establishments, at each of which I had broken the record for insolence and academic incompetence, I finally found myself at "the Marais", an Institute in Paris, studying for my A–level. I was 19 years old and already two years behind schedule.

At the institute I found teachers who were passionate about their work, and who were able to communicate that passion. They were close to their students and were prepared to give them time. For the first time in my life I felt comfortable in a classroom. I learned to like school. I was still restless, but I felt an obligation to show the same respect to the teachers that they had shown me, and that they had shown for their work. I was even respectful towards the director of the institute, an impressive man but someone who was feared by everyone.

One day, when I was talking to the person I was sitting alongside in class, another student shouted out to me: "Mouratoglou, shut up!" He had exposed me in front of everybody. I don't handle provocation well. I replied tit for tat: "If my girlfriend did look like yours I would shut up." He was spitting mad... and much bigger than me. I suspected that it would all end in violence. We met when we left the classroom. He took both my hands into his and crushed them. I did not protest. I stared at him, my face just a few centimetres from his. Other students jumped in between us and only just managed to separate us. It was no surprise that I found myself in the office of the institute's director. He demanded an explanation. I told him the whole story. He said: "In your place I would have smashed his face in, but do me a favour and do that away from these premises." I thought he was a great guy.

In this environment, where I felt respected, I got a taste for my studies and became a good pupil. I had some potential and at last I had found a structure in which I wanted to learn.

I was therefore in a position where I was trying to make up for lost time. I was a complete fool, with no culture and no ideas. I wasn't even sure that I could have pointed a finger at France on a map of the world. From then on I gave everything. I spent hours reading, discovering, learning. True to form, I went from zero to one hundred in a fraction of a second. I wanted to know and understand everything about the outside world. I devoured every book I could lay my hands on, I played music, I sang and I was passionate about jazz guitar. Two years later I entered the best music school in Paris, the CIM, to complete my training. I decided that I wanted to perform in concert and immediately set about the task. I played in several concerts as the leader of my band. I combined the roles of manager (it was me who organised our bookings), leader, singer, musician, and even often arranger. However, I did not look on it as a job. I had too much ground to make up, I had started too late and there was clearly a different path ahead.

For the following seven years I dug my racket out of the cupboard five times a year, at the insistence of my friends, to play in team matches for my club.

On the morning of these matches I would arrive

having slept only three hours after staying out late the previous night. I did not practise at all. I no longer stuck to any sort of discipline on a physical level. All my mates thought that my opponents would murder me. I even used to light up a cigarette just before going on court. But once we started I would be out there playing serve-and-volley and impossible to pass at the net. I hit some unlikely volleys and some exquisite half-volleys. My mates were captivated. They called me The Artist. Tennis continued to carry me on its shoulders. Unbelievable.

> *"I am the master of my destiny,*
> *the captain of my soul."*
> William Ernest Henley

Something essential was still missing from my life. At the end of the first round I had conquered my own body; at the end of the second I had won my freedom. However, I still struggled when it came to connecting with other people.

I still suffered from great shyness. I was nearly ready to meet life full on, but I was still only "nearly ready". I had to solve this problem, which had weighed me down for too long. I had acquired a good degree of confidence along the route I had already covered. However, one last obstacle stood between me and my dreams, and I could not tolerate that any more. I would pay whatever price was needed to resolve this problem.

I remember the day, when I was still an adolescent, when I went to my mother to discuss this problem: "I feel ill at ease with people. I don't know what to say to them. I am so nervous amongst people I don't know that I find it impossible to be myself – and as a result I avoid any situations like that. I know that I have a mental block about this and I'm not getting over it. Do you have any ideas as to how I can get over this?" She replied: "Yes, the best thing is to seek help. The best option is probably to go and see a psychoanalyst."

I took mother's advice and sought therapy, which would carry on for ten years.

When I arrived on the first day I didn't have a clue about what to expect. When I asked the psychotherapist for some details he replied: "It's very simple: you are sitting in a moving train. Describe the landscape to me." I was after an immediate solution but this was just a waste of time. The first year was painful. I went to his surgery once a week. I sat opposite him. Ideas bounced around my head but I could not express them. I tried to sort it out because I wanted to "find" something to say to him, but, clearly, there was nothing. It felt the same as when I was face to face with someone I didn't know. As a result, I said nothing. I didn't want to come across as a nobody. I didn't want to slip into banalities. I built a shell around myself and refrained from offering up the slightest personal titbit, which might have put me in a position of weakness. It was a completely senseless approach to take, when undergoing psychotherapy. I was refusing to give him any opportunity to make a negative judgement about me. To quote the wise words of Sacha Guitry: *"Better keep your mouth shut and appear stupid than to open it and remove all doubt."*

This circus went on for a whole year, one weekly session after another. Every time I came away fuming with anger. I hated myself for being so worthless, for being unable to talk. On the way home I roared out in resentment. I promised myself that I would break this cycle, but the scenario kept repeating itself.

However, these sessions, always finishing in my obstinate silence, were not without their worth. Little by little I started to understand this mental block which was stopping me communicating with other people. I was afraid of silence; in trying at all costs to break this silence I was paralysing myself. I have learned to conquer this and today I know how to use it wisely. When you are with someone, being able to take charge of the silence is a valuable asset; it allows you to hear and it invites the other person to open up. Besides, when you are involved in any negotiations, is it not said that the first person who talks is the one who loses?

As the sessions went by, I learned to put what I was thinking into words. I let them come to me.

After a year, a sound came out of my mouth. It was certainly banal, but it didn't matter: I was finally expressing myself, which was a huge victory. Things were beginning to change at last. My psychotherapist ended the session by saying this: "This year of silence will be part of the story of your analysis."

I was proud of myself. At last I would be able to grow. I started to understand that it is largely through our experiences that we build ourselves. They influence what we will do in future. They condition our reflexes. If, for example, someone panics in a stressful situation, he or she will conclude that they don't know how to handle stress. If this happens again several times, they will be convinced of it and that belief will become an absolute and unarguable reality. The only way of breaking this type of vicious circle is to programme yourself by artificially recreating the situation in which you failed in order to find a positive outcome.

Positive experiences make us grow. They reinforce our own confidence. They enable us to trust in our own abilities. If we come to associate a difficult situation with a positive feeling, we grow. In the opposite case, we persuade ourselves that we cannot handle the situation. When we need to face up to these circumstances we instead develop strategies to avoid them. In my own case I've been able to conquer situations which had always beaten me in the past. I refused to accept fate. I had lost once, twice, a hundred times, a thousand times, but I stuck at it because I was convinced that I would win in the end.

From that famous day when a word finally came out of my mouth during a session, I put faith in myself. I lost no time in stepping into the breach which I had opened. I still faced many potential pitfalls in the course of this long journey of what amounted to personal psycho–analysis, but I had claimed the victory that I had been waiting for – the victory that would give me the courage to stand up to myself.

Having earned my A–Level certificate, I joined a business school. As I did not have any other objective in mind since I had stopped playing tennis, I chose a course of studies which would be the most consistent with my education: business studies. Every evening, after classes, I rushed to my "Fame"–style music school. I was continuing my education in these two different fields. Every day I would switch from the one to the other, which was quite a culture shock. I was obviously more passionate about jazz than I was about economics or accountancy. I regularly appeared in concert and it was at such an event that I met my first wife. I married at the age of 23. A year later she gave birth to Raphael, my first child. Meeting her made me want to settle down and make a living. I decided to give up my studies and enter real life.

I was ready to take the first job which came up, but I did not have any qualifications. My father suggested that I entered his business to learn a trade. He warned me: I would not be given any favourable treatment and I would start at the bottom of the ladder. If I had been handed the Labours of Hercules I would not have been spared anything. I worked in his business for five years. In that time I learned the basics that I would need to set up my own business. I was there for ten or twelve hours a day and was paid a trainee's wage. That was the deal and I happily accepted it because I liked the start-up nature of the company. I was constantly challenged to surpass myself and I wanted to do well.

I spent a whole year just doing accountancy, then management control the following year. Finally I was given practical experience, working under a young shark who was ten years older than me. I adored this guy, who didn't let me get away with anything. He set himself up as my "coach". We had some good times and we both appreciated each other, but he always kept his distance and was very demanding of me. He taught me how to work and taught me all the basic principles of business. He knew that to get the best out of me he needed to set the bar very high. His work was quite diverse, from the management of real estate to setting up new businesses, according to models pre-established by my father, to whom he reported directly.

At that time the company bought one property dealer's entire housing stock and we were in charge of ensuring the profitability of every plot. They included two low rent hotels which were so grim they were beyond classification. Situated in the heart of Paris, they were like council flats. A couple of hundred illegal immigrants lived there in about eighty rooms. Our mission was a hard one. In the mid–term, it consisted of organising the work that needed to be done to turn them into hotels. However, in the short term, as we waited for the finance, we had to collect the rents in order to pay our own monthly bills.

The company clearly liked a sporting challenge! On several occasions my buddy and I, found ourselves in the caretaker's lodge on the telephone to the police station. Behind the doors the residents, weapons in hand, were ready to greet us. The caretaker, who was a hardened political refugee from the Comoros Islands, regularly got beaten up.

Our "clientele" essentially consisted of drug traffickers and pimps, most of them former convicts. As you can imagine settling a rent bill was not very high on their list of priorities. You therefore had to argue with them, putting across the message that you were strong and sure of yourself, but at the same time not allowing tempers to rise. The police refused to visit the upper levels of the building, which they judged to be too dangerous, except when there were incidents surrounding the settlement of bills, for which they would turn up in numbers.

We did that for a whole year. It was an emotional time. Every morning I would go to the office with a knot in my stomach and with my insides in turmoil.

After a year we were finally given another task. Our replacements, who were two "professionals" in this type of work and looked like bouncers, lasted one week. One of them, who was stabbed in the knee, would suffer the after-effects for the rest of his life.

Once this adventure was over, my training continued with a more traditional form of property management. The company owned several properties which comprised buildings and flats. My partner told me that I was now ready to go forward on my own and to take on responsibilities. I decided to set up an agency, which would take care of the management of rents for the entire housing stock. As it was self–financing, I had the idea of also conducting property deals through the agency to improve its profitability. The figures quickly took off, enabling me to open a small chain of agencies, three in total.

Parallel with this activity, my father was moving into the field of renewable energy: hydro–electric power stations, solar panels and finally wind farms. He set himself up in France's overseas departments: Guadeloupe, Martinique and La Reunion. A system of fiscal incentives designed to improve the production of energy in the overseas departments made it possible to develop an area of business that had not hitherto been profitable.

With my senior colleague, I managed the on–site operations. Our job was to negotiate with the local manufacturers, to find suitable sites, to keep track of the installation work and then maintain the projects. I went regularly to Guadeloupe.

The subsidiary company for renewable energy flourished and took on an increasing importance. The next year I was entrusted with responsibility for hundreds of solar power projects. I had the feeling that I had covered everything in this area. The machine was up and running, my team were on top of the subject and I had a lot of spare time.

My wife and I separated after a year of marriage. Nevertheless, I am proud of the fact that I have maintained an excellent relationship with her. She is still my lawyer and we are in regular contact about our son.

It was at that time that I got out my racket again. The passion was back... I practised three or four times a week and I made myself do some physical training in the evenings. I did that by myself in the Bois de Boulogne in the middle of winter. I decided to hire the services of a coach. I played in some tournaments, just for the pleasure of competing, although not very often as I was busy elsewhere. I had actually just met the woman who was to become my second wife.

With a professional life that was operating on auto–pilot and with tennis having pulled me back into its web, I decided to set up a little organisation to accommodate players of all ages and all levels. The coach who was working with me at this time and myself, found a club in the Parisian suburb of Colombes which agreed to host us. I put an advert in *Tennis Magazine* and in January 1996 I welcomed my first clients. They were thirty–year–old club players who were keen to move up a gear. The Tennis Competition Training Team (TETC) was born. Within six months we had about twenty clients, but despite this I still kept up with my work in renewable energy.

> *"He who walks in someone else's*
> *tracks never leaves a mark."*
>
> Chinese proverb

A year later, at the age of twenty-seven, I prepared to go through a decisive turning point in my future career as a coach.

Eleven years after that famous meeting with my parents, which had sounded the death knell for my tennis adventure, I found myself again face to face with my father, in his office, in order to talk about the future. I did not want this meeting to go wrong, because the first one had cost me dear. I was a different person now. The shy and unconfident adolescent had given way to a man who was determined and sure of himself.

My father began the conversation: "You have worked in my company for six years now and you have proved yourself. You are ready. The business has grown a lot. We have some big projects ahead and I would like you to be part of them. We can start to build some businesses together. You are ready to work alongside me."

I was flattered and proud. I knew the hardships that I had been through, the efforts I had made, and the results I had achieved. His proposal showed that he too was aware of that and his recognition touched me deeply.

But I had other projects in hand. I replied to him: "Thank you very much for your proposal. But tennis is my life. I am lucky enough to have a real passion for it and I want to live it. I haven't recovered from the enormous frustration that I felt. I could not get to the highest level as a player. I want to see what it's like there in another way, by taking other players to the top. I am not a coach, so the only way for me to achieve that is via a tennis academy. I have set up a little organisation which is profitable and from now onwards I want to make it grow. I would like to help young people to live the dream that I was unable to."

"When I am your age, I want to look back on my life and to be proud of what I have accomplished. I know that building some electric power stations would not satisfy me."

"To be gripped by a passion like this is something of incalculable good fortune. I want to live that passion to the full. I need emotion in my life. I did need to throw myself one hundred per cent into it. Tennis will bring me that. I am therefore going to have to turn down your offer."

"Very well. I understand. Can I help you? And if so, how?"

"It's quite simple. I need funds for two projects. Firstly I want to recruit a top coach, someone who is recognised in his field, who will help me to convince young players with potential to come and work in my organisation. Then I need financial backing for the group of talented players that I will have selected."

"Very good. Draw up a business plan and I will look at it with you."

I had turned a huge corner. I had taken a major decision over my future and my father had agreed to go along with it. Now it was a case of making it happen.

At the end of this conversation I felt stunned. I was filled with admiration for my father, who had listened to me and understood me. Above all I was relieved that I had not blown my rendez–vous with my own history.

In putting this meeting in perspective with the one we'd had eleven years previously, I realised that my parents would have been just as prepared to listen to me at that time. It was me, who had been unable to sell my sporting project to them. This discovery came as a shock to me. I could picture the scene from eleven years previously, but the perception that I had of it was very different. I had been unable to convince my parents, who loved me, to help me accomplish the thing that was dearest to my heart. My reaction was simply the result of my inability to understand what was obvious. I had shifted the problem on to them in order not to call myself into question. I had mistaken the enemy: the only person who had been responsible for my giving up tennis was me.

My parents had feared that my passion for tennis would just be a passing phase and I had not been able to reassure them that was not the case. They doubted my potential; I should have made them believe in me. They were concerned for my future; I could have suggested a career path, which would have included time for my education. I had failed to see the real reasons for their refusal and had not come up with the responses that would have swung the balance in my favour.

This lesson only strengthened my growing certainty that my future depended only on myself, on my ability to convince, to train, to work, to plan. I realised that shifting the blame on to others would be a major stumbling block to my development because it would stop me learning from my mistakes. That day I made myself a number of promises:

My future would be entirely in my own hands.

I will seek what I need in order to get what I want.

I will learn to convince other people and to share my vision with them.

I will not allow choices that other people make to be an obstacle to my own objectives. And above all…

I will learn a lesson from each one of my failures.

By the time I reached forty I would be one hundred times better at following these precepts. I would adopt Roosevelt's formula: "Winners find a way. Losers find an excuse." I would see to it that I no longer needed excuses.

4
The day when I became a coach

"Great souls have wills, feeble ones have only wishes."
Chinese proverb

My academy was up and running, but I felt far from fulfilled by it. I wanted my players to develop at the highest level. In order for that to happen, we needed the very best material, young people who would be capable of reaching the top. The point was that I did not know the best young players and they had never heard of me. I had no reputation. I therefore had the idea of approaching someone from the world of coaching, who would be known by everyone, the Australian Bob Brett. At the end of the 1990s he had distinguished himself by first taking Boris Becker to number one in the world and then guiding Goran Ivanišević to number two. He had the wind in his sails. He was the coach of the moment.

If only my academy could bear his name I would gain the credibility that would enable me to recruit young players who appealed to me in terms of their potential. At the time I was thinking about him he started working with a highly promising young German player, Nicolas Kiefer.

When I went to the "Larrère" shop in Paris to get my rackets strung I met one of his fellow countrymen, John Elliot. I got on well with him and asked him if by any chance he knew Bob Brett. He said he did. I then asked if he could organise a meeting for me. The meeting took place in 1998, during the French Open, at the hotel where Brett was staying during the tournament.

"They didn't know it was impossible so they did it."
Oscar Wilde

I had an hour to convince him about my project. It was more than I would need. I walked into the hotel full of enthusiasm and confidence. I saw this meeting as a challenge. I had the honour of meeting this man for whom I had infinite respect and the opportunity to make him my ally. I was so keen that I did not consider for a single moment that I did not actually have any trump cards to play in order to win him over. I was young, inexperienced and unknown in the world of tennis. What was more, I did not have any infrastructure and I could not give him any financial guarantees. The least you could say was that, on paper, my project did not look serious. I would draw a new lesson from this experience: the reality of events and situations is of only limited importance; the only thing that matters, is the perception you have of them. Bob Brett is a great man, but I did not get flustered. I showed that I was enthusiastic, spirited, appealing. I had confidence in my ability to raise my own game and touch a chord within him that would turn things in my favour.

Besides, I had done my homework for this meeting. I had done my research, I knew Brett's story, I had an idea of his philosophy and his objectives. I knew how to talk to him, how to show him the benefits that he could derive from my project.

And I hit the bull's eye. After we had talked for an hour, Bob stood up and offered his hand to me: "I'm with you. Deal done. We'll meet again after Wimbledon. Prepare the contract and I'll sign it then."

The meeting was set up, but now there was all the work to do. A project like that needed a spacious site, a team of coaches who would do the right things and a group of promising players. I had three months and no idea of how I was going to achieve this feat. However, I was calm. The idea of this alliance with Brett filled me with courage and determination. Being free of all other professional constraints, I dedicated myself entirely to the project. After Wimbledon the Australian coach signed my contract without even having had the

read it (it was drawn up in French). He
complete trust in me. I spent the summer
looking for a club with the right facilities, which
would be able to accommodate us. I set my heart
on a place at Montreuil, in Seine–Saint–Denis.
Three months later the Bob Brett Academy was
born.

I owed a lot to Bob. Firstly because he put his
trust in me, secondly because he liked me, and
finally because he taught me all the basics of my
profession. He had turned a deaf ear to those
professional people in tennis who had warned him:
"How can you trust someone unknown like that?
He's nothing in tennis." Bob himself agreed to
come to Montreuil, where I had taken up residence.
He praised my energy, my determination and my
hard work. In a certain manner of speaking he
protected me.

The next six years were exciting. I lived my
dream: identifying future champions and getting
the group to work in a "start–up" environment.
Bob was great with me. He always insisted on me
going on court with him to help him in his work.
Even though he was only there fifty days a year, he
left me with a mine of information after every visit.
I brought together a phenomenal group of talented
young people. To name just a few: Paul–Henri
Mathieu, Marcos Baghdatis, Gilles Muller, Pauline
Parmentier, Sergei Stakhovsky, Ivo Karlovic, Mario
Ancic, Petra Cetkovska, Mandy Minella, Dudi Sela

and Hicham Arazi. All rubbed shoulders at our site.

I put in place a system, which satisfied everybody. I paid for the player's training and in return the player gave me a percentage of his prize money (from tournaments) until he had paid for the cost of his training. The only problem was that if a player did not reach the top level I would not recoup my investment. It was in order to alleviate this problem that I set up a sports management structure in 2000. I aligned myself with Laurent Rizzo, who at the time worked for Advantage International, which would later become Octagon, one of the most important companies in the field of athlete representation. We represented our players and took a percentage from their sponsorship contracts. I thereby covered my expenses and at the same time did some great PR work on behalf of our most brilliant trainees.

Working alongside Laurent, I learned a new profession, which also made good use of my business training. Our roles were clearly defined. His job was to sign up the players and negotiate their endorsement contracts, mine was to give them what they needed to be winners. I thereby identified a number of future champions. We signed up Marion Bartoli when she was just 16 – totally unknown Caroline Wozniacki at the age of 10 and Marcos Baghdatis at 13. We missed out on lot of promising young players as we lacked credibility compared with the big companies. In particular I identified Juan Martin del Potro when he was 12, Fernando Verdasco as a Junior likewise Stan Wawrinka but we were unable to get them over the line. Laurent and I have a common credo: everything is possible. Nevertheless I decided in 2007 to end this line of business. Handling both the management and the training of my players was a heavy weight on my shoulders.

Besides, the big management companies have become ruthless rivals. They stopped their players coming to train at the academy because they feared that we would persuade them to leave in order to sign up with our own sports management business… and they were right. Our project had become counter–productive, because my passion was being out there on the practice court and I wanted to work with the best players. There were many who dreamed of teaming up with us but were unable to make that step.

I therefore took the decision to dissolve the sporting management structure and Laurent joined Paris Saint Germain Merchandising as their Managing Director. We are still friends to this day.

This period was particularly trying. I was fighting a lone battle against everybody. The world of French tennis was self–perpetuating. It was comprised of people who had been there for decades. I was a determined little newcomer who got in the way. People looked on my progress with disapproval. The French Tennis Federation considered me a spoilsport who dared to challenge its hegemony on French soil.

Learning that a number of French number ones were training with me, some representatives of the federation turned up at the academy one day. They took up position beside the courts, in the middle of training, and started to take notes. I was shocked by their totally disrespectful methods. That, for me, was symptomatic of the feeling of absolute power which these people had. I went over to see them and told them to leave the courts. When we got outside I crossed the t's and dotted the i's: "You're at my place. When you arrive at someone's property, you knock before going in, someone opens the door and then you ask if you can enter and sit down. You don't knock down the door in order to go and sit in someone's living room." If someone tries to use force against me I will shut the door in their face. Temperamentally I am not aggressive, but a lack of respect appals me more than anything.

These ups and downs did not prevent me from making progress with my academy. I fed on all the hatreds and jealousies of which I was an object. Far from discouraging me, they gave me the strength to move forward.

Brett, as my spiritual father, proudly passed on to me his coaching knowledge. I absorbed it like a sponge. It was fortunate that I knew nothing because that allowed me to be open–minded. I wanted to learn everything. From this perspective I devoured all the coaching books which were on the market. I particularly discovered the ones by Tony Robbins, which reinforced and strengthened my own vision of coaching. I grew immeasurably through Bob's teaching and always wanted more. I worked relentlessly, I managed the recruitment of players and coaches, I planned the training programmes and I analysed the results. I talked to everyone and I put a lot of pressure on the players and the coaches in terms of winning matches. Having suffered so much at school, under the aegis of an educational structure which judged me and rejected me, I now understood the importance of a kindly figure of authority.

The years of training are crucial in the development of young people. It's at that time that they prepare for life. I was shocked by the treatment of those who did not fall into line, those who did not fill the classic criteria. The French school model is too negative, based too much on repression. Children are judged and put in boxes. I remember what the director of the Institut du Marais (the school that made me love school) had told my parents: "Your son is very creative. He has a huge interior world inside him. Mentally he is not always with us. He will follow a profession in which he will be able to exploit this creativity." It was the first time that someone in education had understood me and saw me in positive terms. That

episode allowed me to transform totally my vision
of school and to throw myself into the development
of young people who were in my charge. At last I
was going to be able to give.

*"In theory there is no difference between theory and
practice. In practice, there is."*

Anonymous

From 1998 to 2004, Bob and I operated at 100
miles an hour, in total collusion. Unfortunately my
relationship with the Australian coach deteriorated
towards the end of this period. He visited less and
less frequently, did a huge amount of travelling on
the circuit with Nicolas Kiefer, whom he had finally
managed to take to number four in the world. From
my point of view I had 40 players to look after and
plenty of training questions to solve. I wanted to
make progress and I intervened when coaches ran
into problems. I often sought outside help,
especially in terms of mental preparation. I offered
to my coaches the assistance of a mental coach
through some training seminars. That made Bob
see red. I explained to him that I couldn't just wait
for his return with my arms crossed, doing nothing.
I said I had to move forward and help everyone to
progress. But he saw this initiative as a piece of
treachery, a conspiracy against him. He even went
so far as to tell me: "No one has ever humiliated me
like that. It's as if my wife had been unfaithful to

me." I was surprised by this analogy which seemed to me to be out of place and over the top. He was beside himself, but he did not make an impression on me. He raised his voice in vain because I was totally behind my own decision. I did not come to regret it.

It was then that he gave me an ultimatum: "It's the Bob Brett Academy. I want to be in complete control of it. I'll be here 150 days a year. I'm no longer with Kiefer so I have the time to devote to it. Take it or leave it." If I disregarded the financial problem – I would need to unlock some resources to pay for Bob's extra 100 days at the Academy – the idea delighted me. Who better than Bob Brett himself to run the academy which bore his name? There was no better coach and nobody knew tennis better than him. I accepted without hesitation.

What appeared obvious in theory actually proved to be a real catastrophe in practice. The players had been used to a certain form of management – mine. I put them under constant pressure, but I managed both the players and the coaches in a humane way. Bob chose to impose his very autocratic style without taking into account anyone's feelings. He antagonised everyone and the atmosphere quickly deteriorated. The staff were worn out. Over the course of eight months several players left us, including Ivo Karlovic and Gilles Muller. Marcos himself, my spiritual son, who had become world junior champion and had just broken into the world's top 200 on the ATP rankings, told me he was unhappy and talked about leaving eventually. I could not allow myself to let him leave. I resolved to talk to Bob: "A lot of people are unhappy and we are losing the players one by one. We can't carry on like this. Either you have to change your ways or our partnership is going to have to end. Everything that I have built over the last six years is going up in smoke."

With his ego as a coaching superstar, he obviously could not put up with such talk from a 34–year–old upstart who had learned everything from him. He left the academy on the spot. I watched him leave with a mixture of relief and sadness. I owed him a lot, but I could not allow myself to put everything in peril. I settled the matter for once and for all.

His managerial style could no doubt have worked, but for that to happen it would have been necessary to impose it from the start. It was the sudden and radical change of methods that antagonised the whole group. Besides, I think that Bob made more of it simply because he had been annoyed by decisions I had made. He is a man of great finesse. I'm convinced that if he hadn't been blinded by emotion he would have sensed that this sudden and extreme managerial about–turn was going to take us into a position of failure and he would have changed the way he dealt with people.

Bob's hasty departure marked the start of a new

era. I suffered following our split and I was on the point of letting everything slip away. But a discussion with Marcos and his father put my ideas back in place. "You must not stop, Patrick. The players trust you. We follow you 100 per cent. Rely on us and carry on with the adventure." They knew how to find the words to touch me. I felt loved and this encouragement restored my faith. Looking on it with detachment, I don't think that I would have cracked. I needed time to manage. When he left, Bob announced to the players at the academy that he was setting up his own organisation in Italy. He suggested they should join him there. When they came to warn me about this and assured me of their unconditional support I felt reinvigorated and ready to bounce back.

How would the organisation cope without the name Bob Brett before the word "Academy"? Would the players still have faith in me? Would I have enough credibility to recruit players? The questions were bouncing around. I had to rename the organisation. I flirted with the idea of taking on another well-known coach and putting his name to it. But I hesitated about making a long-term investment based on the image of someone who could disappear at any moment. It had worked the first time around, with Bob taking me under his wing, but I had no idea what would become of the academy without this prestigious name attached to it. I therefore decided to rename the organisation the TETC Academy, which had the undoubted advantage of granting me complete freedom to do what I wanted. On the other hand the name did not mean anything to anybody and I would have to build the whole image of the place.

It was when I was grappling with those questions that I had lunch with one of my partners and friends, Philippe Sautet. We had set up together Once Upon A Time Tennis (OUATT), a junior tournament notable for the fact that the draws were made according to years of birth. It is still the tournament that attracts the biggest number of young players across the world.

Philippe tried to convince me that it was imperative that I attached my own name to the organisation. "Every academy in the world is represented by a man whose image is associated with it. He embodies the values of the organisation. Look at Bollettieri, Sanchez–Casal, Evert etc. You have done all the work for years. You are the TETC Academy. Call it Mouratoglou's." His argument was convincing and I made my decision. The TETC Academy became the Mouratoglou Tennis Academy. Now I had to build an image, because from this moment onwards our destinies were tied together. I was going to have to go on the court and have my name linked to results. I wanted to become the best coach in the world! It was time to go out there and prove what I had learned from Bob Brett. Besides, I had one advantage that should not be dismissed: I had no pre-conceived ideas. I was not going out there to reassure myself or to hide behind techniques or tactics that I had learned. I had only one idea in my head: to get results. I was not after coaching certificates and I had no lust for power. I just had a great desire for my gamble to come off. My player and I were in the same boat: my success would inevitably come through his.

Two years later my academy was in full swing. We left Montreuil because I wanted to build an infrastructure that would meet my needs perfectly.

I am very proud of the results that we achieved: since 1996 we had developed dozens of players whom we had taken towards the top of world tennis. On twelve occasions our youngsters had reached junior Grand Slam finals and three of them had earned the title of junior world champion. Out of this group, more than twenty had broken into the world's top 100. Some had made the top 20, even the top 10. They have won a number of titles on the circuit, including the Grand Slam titles won by Serena Williams.

In 2014 we gave ourselves the means of going even higher, thanks to the acquisition of the Sophia Country Club in the French Riviera. The next step in the adventure is the building of the biggest training centre in Europe. From now onwards it would be in this place and with this exceptional asset that my academy would blossom.

As for me, I had become a coach. The

development of my academy was directly linked to my own personal journey. My credibility as a coach would strengthen the reputation of my organisation. I had to be very successful. There could be no other way. I did not bring much with me. I had not been a great player, I was not a great technician and nor was I a tactical specialist. O n the other hand, I had been taught the basics of my profession by Bob, and my hyper-sensitiveness, which had been put to the test by the difficulties of my youth, had taught me how to read people. I had huge motivation, a winning culture and common sense.

5
What is coaching?

"Benefiting from coaching is not an admission of weakness, but the acknowledgement of potential."
Anonymous

In the course of these twenty years of rich experiences, I have come to understand, through my daily work, the essential differences between a trainer and a coach. In everyday parlance these two terms are often confused; worse still, the word "coach" is brought into disrepute. Certain excellent trainers make wretched coaches and vice versa. It's rare for people to be able to do both jobs well. Yet it is the ability to bring together these two sets of skills that determines the success or otherwise of a player.

A trainer is someone who analyses the strengths and weaknesses of his player, then puts in place a development strategy for his game. He then carries that out every day on the practice court.

In tournaments he is familiar with his player's

opponents and knows their strengths and weaknesses. Before every match he draws up a tactical plan designed to exploit any weaknesses in the opponent's game.

The coach is the person who manages the group of people who constitute the team around the player. He's a generalist who does not specialise in either physical preparation or medical science but understands both areas well enough to call on the technical skills of others when he thinks the player needs their interventions. He knows how to bring together and manage a team. He establishes a privileged connection with the player, integrating himself into his world in order to understand his inner self. He gives his student a better understanding of his objectives and develops his mind, whereas a trainer is basically working with technical and tactical tools: One is working on the player as a machine while the other is working on him as a human being.

Through the quality of his perception, the coach will help his player to mobilise the resources he needs to produce a successful outcome. He teaches him to control his emotions, he reinforces his confidence and brings into play the levers which will enable him to take the decisions which will lead to victory.

In being with the player at tournaments throughout the year, he makes sure that the player is in a "state of excellence" and helps him to surpass himself in the most important matches of his career.

"Victory is hidden in the details."

The great coaches in sport are acutely aware of all the parameters that influence results. They know they must master them; failing to master just one of them can result in defeat. There are many and they are diverse: there are a thousand reasons why you win any match over the course of a year, but equally there are a thousand details that can make you lose.

The demands put on a player must be pushed to the limit. It's imperative that we think of everything, because ignoring even the tiniest detail might result in failure. Firstly we need to gather all the information about our own player, process it and then work out our priorities. Finally the coach has to make his own intervention, in the most efficient way possible, in order to obtain the anticipated result. Throughout the process we must remain in control of everything. Every match demands the best possible preparation in order to give us every chance of success. Every training session fits into a long–term plan with regards to the development of our player, but the sessions are also a chance to take the player out of his comfort zone to help him improve.

I love soccer and I am always struck by the merry-go-round of coaches from one club to another year after year. The obvious conclusion is that results do not depend on the coaches, because from one year to the next they have good seasons, average seasons and bad seasons and the cycle invariably seems to repeat itself. They are probably very good soccer technicians, but their options on the field are regularly undermined by any number of details, which might have escaped them or by failings in man-management. While for the most part they do a good job as trainers, they are lacking key elements in terms of coaching. At the same time I can only admire the ability of coaches who are able to exploit to the full the potential of their players. When he arrived at Inter Milan he took charge of what was, on paper, a quality team. When he left the club all the players had become superstars. He successfully brought out the essence from every one of them. In becoming winners they all improved individually.

Victory is crucial in terms of making the improvements that you see in training effective and in ensuring that those improvements are taken on board by the player.

The coach has to get himself into a mind frame where in the mid-term he helps the player develop the weapons he will need tomorrow but also ensures short-term success in terms of results of matches. That is what constitutes a winning combination.

Returning to soccer, how many trainers get

results no matter what team they are in charge of? You can count them on the fingers of one hand. Even then some would say those people are successful only because they are systematically put in charge of the best teams. But that's not right. Even the best teams in the world can have bad seasons. Besides, they have much higher objectives than most other teams.

In the world of tennis, equally, only a very small number of coaches get indisputably good results with every player they work with. Victories, titles and progress up the rankings are the only yardsticks by which the quality of their work can be measured.

In order to achieve excellence in this profession it is vital to take responsibility for every result, whatever the outcome. Accepting that you are the one and only person responsible (for victories as well as defeats) enables you to call yourself into question on a regular basis, which can only be beneficial. I often hear coaches say that they are simply "accompanists" and that their contribution amounts to no more than ten or twenty per cent. What better way of avoiding pressure? You suffer less disappointment when you fail and subsequently you do not call yourself into question as much. This refusal to take on responsibility is one of the main reasons why people do not question one self.

As for the number of obstacles that might

prevent a player being successful, they are potentially infinite. They can cover a whole range of issues: personal matters, relationships, behaviour, as well as physical, technical, tactical or medical problems. Most often it's a subtle combination of all these areas, because there are potential problems in every field.

> *"The real happiness is in looking for it."*
> Jules Renard

There are two sorts of coaches: those who complain about their player, about his deficiencies or his environment, and those who get results thanks to their ability to adapt and find solutions.

Judging people is the worst thing a coach can do, but unfortunately some do it all the time. In making any observation to a player you should consider the following question: will it have a positive effect or, to the contrary, will it be an obstacle to getting the result that you both want?

How many times have we all heard a trainer complain that his player is not listening to him? I always want to reply: "It's your job to make yourself heard. Sort yourself out so that the player wants to listen to you." When he deplores his player's attitude, I ask him if it's because it offends his values or if it's because it gets in the way of his player's success. And I take it as my duty to remind the coach that any behaviour that isn't going to help produce results, needs to be modified and that any behaviour which might not please you, but which brings success should be encouraged. How do you go about that? With every player there is a different way of going about it. There is always a solution. Our job is all about finding it, then putting it into action.

Ever since the start of my career I have always asked myself after my player has lost: "What could I have done differently? In practice, in the warm–up before the match, in my pre–match briefing? Did my player fail to follow the tactics? Was my player in the right state to play? Was there an area of his game which failed him? Was the opponent able to exploit one of my player's weaknesses and if so how could we have avoided that? Where did I go wrong?"

It is through adopting this state of mind, through this assumption of responsibility for the player's result, that you can call everything into question and make progress.

In this world there is no school for tennis coaching. It is a complex profession which requires multiple competences that makes it all the more fascinating. Coaching is absolutely not about imparting knowledge. Coaching is about getting a result, about finding the required solutions through ever–changing means in order to achieve the desired outcomes.

The arrival of mental coaches in sport is a

response to this weakness among trainers. Lacking in certain areas, they try to redeem themselves by calling on these outside influences in the belief that this is an area, which is beyond their abilities and outside their field of competence. Yet this is at the very heart of their profession. When this course of action does not come from the coaches it often comes from a player's parents, who judge that there has been a failure and that the coach has been unable to come up with a solution. These excellent technicians do not know how to intervene on a human level. Yet it is the coach who is best placed to do this. The coach is living alongside the player every day, has all the necessary information, has the confidence of his student, and has a natural authority over the player.

The player does not demand that the coach holds "good practice sessions". Instead he wants the coach to help him to climb up the ladder and to overcome difficulties.

The tennis player is a complex machine, with all manner of working parts. Achieving the results you desire requires an understanding of the whole system. The coach is the only person who has all the pieces of the puzzle. He needs to have the means to put them together and to intervene in all the areas where he judges it necessary to achieve the desired results. In order to achieve that he must be prepared.

"To write is to think twice."

In my philosophy, results are what count. Because of that I have over the years collected all sorts of information that could be useful to me in helping my players to progress or to win important matches.

I began by writing in notebooks. Today my cupboards are filled with dozens and dozens of notebooks. In them are my plans for training sessions, my analyses of opponents, my feelings at the time and statistics compiled during competitions. Before delivering a pre-match briefing to my players, I take care to write it out several times. That helps me to look more objectively at what I had intended to say and to modify it as necessary.

I have been interested in statistics ever since I took up this profession because I believe that they shed a complementary and essential light on things. The tennis court is a geometric shape and everything that happens on it takes place within mathematical rules, which you must understand and take on board.

Statistics provide you with a view that is entirely rational, cold and unemotional – but also one that is implacable. As an illustration of this, no player can claim that his backhand was "terrible" if the statistics show that he made twice as many errors on his forehand.

Having been unable to use any existing tools, I created my own statistical charts. I spent thousands of hours watching matches while putting crosses in boxes with my pen, so that I could then run them through a computer programme, which I created. This automatically calculates my match statistics from the moment the figures are input.

The statistics complement what I feel and see as a coach. They enable me to verify the accuracy and the validity of my analyses and observations. As coaches we have a responsibility. We give players our verdicts on their performances and we take charge of their work, so it is only right that we show them the proof and the accuracy of our judgements.

I use the same methods to verify (or not) changes to be made in my player's game. For example, if we are working on the effectiveness of the player's use of sliced serves at deuce, I use two or three statistics which will enable me to draw graphs showing how effective they have been over periods of three months, six months and a year. In this particular case I will be interested in his first-serve percentage when he chooses to slice compared to his general first-serve percentage. This will let me know whether it is a serve that he is able to put in court as frequently as his other serves. Then I will be interested in the aces and service winners achieved with this serve compared with the total number of serves he hits in this area. Once again I will compare this statistic with his general serving statistics.

Finally I will study his percentage of points won after such a serve and obviously compare that figure with the total number of other serves hit in other areas.

With all this information compiled match after match it is easy to draw development graphs and to establish in a mathematical manner whether or not we have made progress in those areas of the game where we have been concentrating our efforts.

I equally use statistics to unravel the games of opponents in order to put in place winning strategies against them. When you establish that when a certain player goes break point down he systematically serves on the T and then hits a forehand down the line, you possess a certain advantage against that player. Likewise when you establish, for example, that the player moves backwards as soon as the opponent hits the ball more than a metre above the net on to his backhand.

I now possess files on hundreds of players with winning strategies that I have drawn up against them – particularly through the use of statistics – which I have then put into practice on the court.

We are entering another dimension with the recent emergence of technologies, which bring together video cameras and statistics. With six cameras and a computer in operation, nothing escapes them: the height of the ball as it goes over the net, the reading of angles, the moment of impact when the racket hits the ball, the contact point with the ball in relation to the quality of the opponent's shot, the distance a player covers during a match, the speed of a player running forward or in running from left to right compared with right to left, favourite patterns of play, serves struck according to the score etc. The possible information provided is almost infinite.

One of the keys to the success of these new eldorados will be to know what areas on which to focus the computer in order to produce information that will be interesting and telling. Then there will be work involved in helping to handle that information: it is important to make use of statistics but what do you do with them exactly? What conclusions can I draw from them in terms of my practice sessions? How can I be more efficient? How can I use these keys to beat my opponent?

With the emergence of this technology, the coaching profession is undergoing great changes.

Developing the coaches of tomorrow is a project that I expect to see through. I want to enable trainers to complete their development so that they can use more tools and thereby enhance their performance.

6
My first collaborations

"There is only one way to learn.
It's through action."

Paulo Coelho

In 2004, at the time when Bob Brett left me and the academy became the Mouratoglou Tennis Academy, a 10–year–old boy arrived from New Zealand. He was called Sebastian Lavie. I immediately fell under the charm of his personality, his charisma and his tennis. He was sure of himself, completely hilarious (he always had funny stories to tell and an incredible repartee) and looked like a Californian surfer. He asked me to coach him while he was looking for a trainer. I was initially surprised by this proposal, but it came just at the right time and I accepted. For a year I spent two to three hours a day on the court with Sebastian as I took up the challenge.

A year later, having found a coach for him, I pulled back. I have kept a very strong relationship with Seb. I do have some regrets about him. When his parents returned to New Zealand, when he was 13, he decided to stay in France, at the academy. But after getting to the final of the Petits As tournament, which is a real world championship for the under–14s, his tennis stagnated and did not flourish any more. I understood that he felt abandoned. He had chosen me. He had stayed in France because he had faith in me, yet I was not there for him as I was too involved in other coaching projects, which occupied all my time.

Today I am angry with myself for not having been up to speed with what was happening. When I realised how offhand I had been, I invited him to come and live with me and my children. He went on to live with us for several years. It was my way of showing him that he was part of the family. Today he is 22 and a talented professional coach. He coaches Julia Glushko, a top 100 player.

"Victory has a hundred fathers
but defeat is an orphan."
John Fitzgerald Kennedy

After my first year working with Seb, I made my annual visit to the Orange Bowl in order to watch some players from my academy and to look for some stars of tomorrow. Irena Pavlovic, a fifteen-year-old who had been with us from the age of nine, had some real problems there. She lost in the first round to an opponent who was not very good. Playing badly on a given day can happen to any professional player, but in this case the defeat was a warning signal. Irena was very precocious and had been talked about from a very early age. At the age of eleven, when she was French No. 1 in her age group, she played a flamboyant and high–quality style of tennis. She was ultra–aggressive and played close to the baseline. She reeled off victories and everybody saw her as a future top ten player. However, for the last two years her results had been in decline. She was no longer making progress and had been showing more and more nerves in her matches. She became paralysed by the prospect of defeat. Her father, who had coached her from her earliest years, did not know what to do about it. Sitting down at a table at the Key Biscayne club after the match, Dragan Pavlovic told me coldly, under the tearful eye of his daughter: "I don't know what to do with her any more. She doesn't listen to me any more. She is undisciplined. I leave her with you."

With those words he got up and left. A glacial silence fell over the table. Irena cried. I had known her for six years. I had watched her grow day by day. I was emotionally attached to her. I had also watched her train hard. Irena was in a situation of failure, which in itself was a source of suffering for her. What I had just witnessed seemed to me to be unfair on her, because she had been making every possible effort. How can you reproach someone who gives one hundred per cent but is unable to achieve the results you had been hoping for?

Injustice generates feelings inside me that I find hard to control. It makes me revolt, touches me deeply and prompts me into immediate action.

In the end the father who unloads his frustration on to his child, or the coach who does the same with his student, is no longer filling the role of an educator or of a coach, whose job is to find the solutions to help their charge reach his or her objectives. He is just letting out his frustration at not reaching his goals. He is unloading his anger on to the very person who is needing help. It's a reaction which I could analyse on an intellectual level but which I totally condemn because in every case it is inappropriate and destructive.

I felt saddened for her, even more so because she seemed so fragile. Irena was frail. She still had a face like that of a doll, with big eyes. It seemed as if everything had been taken away from her. Besides, I could not allow myself to let her talent go to waste. I turned towards her and said: "Irena, let's meet on the court at nine tomorrow morning." That was how I came to find myself embarking on a new adventure.

I immediately set myself some goals. I had to bring back her smile and make her value training again. For too long the court had just been synonymous with suffering for her.

I knew what she liked in tennis: she liked hitting the ball hard. At first I set about bringing back her enjoyment in just hitting a ball. After quickly doing some technical work in order to make the ball come off her racket with more power, I would just feed her some balls on which she could demonstrate her power. I would talk positively to her, motivate her, express my admiration for the quality of her game.

When we gathered up the balls or took a break between drills, I took an interest in her history. Irena is from Serbia; her parents fled the war and had to survive in difficult circumstances for several years. Through our discussions, I developed a trusting relationship with her. For the first time, she told her own story. She'd had very little opportunity to do that while shut away in a relationship only with her father. In me she found both someone who would listen and a demanding trainer.

Just being able to open up and to be listened to gave her back a certain vigour. She had such talent! In my career I've seen very few female players capable of hitting the ball with such timing and with such power. Unfortunately, the crisis of confidence that she had been through came out in her physical tension, which stopped the ball coming off her racket as fast as it had in the past. It was imperative for me to rebuild her confidence. That would be the key to success in the second stage of my project with her. If she could free herself from all her extraneous thoughts as she hit the ball, Irena was capable of pulverising her opponents. I then realised that there were two distinct causes of her lack of confidence. The first was obviously linked to the long stretch of defeats she had gone through over a period of three years. The second, and deeper, cause was the direct consequence of her social isolation. She had been spending most of her time only in the company of her father, whose attitude had increasingly hardened as he was confronted by a situation from which he could not find a way out. Lacking solutions, he had made his daughter bear the weight of her defeats and had developed a very negative approach towards her. I had to take the opposite point of view and construct strategies to restore her confidence.

Having found someone who would listen carefully to her, she gave me pieces of information which were of great importance in terms of enabling me to understand her better.

At the end of every day I would send her a long text message in which I would thank her for everything she had achieved. I always wrote that I was fortunate to be able to work with someone as strong and as talented as her. I was convinced: her tennis was a dream! My encouragement was important because I was very demanding in training. I knew that these messages were helping her scars to heal.

> *"Give me six hours to chop down a tree*
> *and I will spend the first four sharpening the axe."*
> Abraham Lincoln

For the moment it was important to create some positive experiences in order to reprogramme her. Irena had suffered too many defeats and too many reprimands. She associated every match with a terrifying experience which ended in a disappointment, undermining her morale and her confidence. Those three years had given her a lot of false ideas which had dragged down her game and her level. She had developed habits which had to be totally reset. The task which I set myself consisted of creating positive experiences which would erase what she had gone through previously. In our daily training sessions I created game situations in which she could shine. I got her to do exercises in which she would spend time inside the court and feel safe there, because she had grown accustomed to positioning herself too far behind the baseline. On the other side of the net I would make sure that I fed her balls which would ensure that each rally ended in a positive outcome.

Every afternoon Irena would win a match in two sets. I started by playing her only against boys as this meant she did not judge her performances as much and would go for her shots more. At the start I lined her up against inferior players and said I didn't mind if she lost so long as she followed certain instructions, such as playing serve-and-volley at least twice in each of her service games. Her tension diminished and her effectiveness grew.

I took great pleasure in seeing the releasing smile which illuminated her face when she enjoyed her first victories in matches against low-level opponents where there was nothing at stake.

After the matches I continued to praise her. I broke down each good shot that she had struck and went into raptures over the power of her hitting. With every day she transformed herself under my very eyes. Now it was time for her to face opponents of higher quality. There were plenty of them at the academy. Before the match I would talk to the players and explain my strategy. I asked them to act normally on the court, but in the end to let her win. They played along with it and Irena continued to gather victories, collecting the scalps of every player at the academy as she went along. Now was the time to beat some female players. I chose the same approach: relying on the confidence Irena had gained, I started by pitting her against opponents who were in theory a lot weaker than her. At the same time I could not ask these opponents to let Irena win because girls are too competitive to accept allowing a rival to beat them.

What was important was that I used the information I had to ensure that she played opponents of a higher quality only when they themselves were lacking confidence. Thanks to this winning combination Irena became increasingly relaxed and was bold enough to step into the court without hesitation and hit the ball.

Eventually I sensed that she was ready to handle proper competition. But it was important to be careful: we did not want to miss the opportunity. I opted for a local tournament in France rather than an international competition as I would be able to control the progress of the opposition in terms of their level. As this was an important tournament in terms of prize money, the greater number of players would also help.

One month before that, my player's level did not rise above 1300 WTA. She went on to beat, in succession, two 1000 WTA, two 500, one 300, one 250 and one 150 WTA. In the end she lost only in the final against Aravane Rezai, who was ranked into the top 100 WTA, in three sets. The transformation was complete. Irena was radiant. But I needed to make sure that I did not get carried away. I told her how proud I was, but I made sure I didn't give any impression that I was surprised. She needed to understand that there was nothing surprising about these victories, because she was a player with a very high level.

In the course of that year she broke into the top 100 of the world juniors, into the top 500 on the WTA and won the French under-16 championships. Nevertheless, there would be a break in our collaboration as another student was demanding my attention... Marcos Baghdatis.

7

Marcos, my spiritual son

I discovered Marcos at the Petits As tournament at Tarbes, which is the official under-14s world championship. It was love at first sight. There was something majestic about his game. He compensated for his fear of not being good enough with total commitment on the court. He alternated between defence and prodigious attacking shots. On several occasions I saw him run round second serves without warning to hit cannonball forehands. It seemed as though a flame burned inside this young player. You could see his *joie de vivre* in his face, which lit up when he smiled. He was a very human individual and his Mediterranean warmth touched me.

I approached his father, who was at the tournament. He went straight to the point: "Marcos must leave Cyprus. There's no way he will succeed if he stays there. There is no infrastructure there, no coaches of the right quality, no rival players to test himself against, no financial means. If he interests you, he's yours. I just want to be sure that you will give him the means so that he has a chance." I did not hesitate for a moment. I so believed in this kid!

This was the year 2000, when we were in Montreuil, a town on the outskirts of Paris, with no living accommodation available. I found a family he could stay with, the Benhaims, who treated him like one of their own children. He was loved, cared for and protected. I came by to pick him up every day in Paris to drive him to the academy. Those long journeys every day helped to strengthen the bonds between us.

I offered Marcos a coach in whom I had a lot of faith, my friend Jean-Paul Damit, who today is the Director of my new academy in Sophia-Antipolis. He has all those rare qualities that make a good coach. He is blessed with real natural authority. A tall and physically very imposing black guy, he has a powerful voice. His physical appearance is the opposite to the sort of person that he is. He has psychological finesse and rare intelligence. He refuses to judge other people and instead always tries to understand and interpret their attitudes. He is hard but fair, demanding and loyal. Above all I love his human values and I know that I can always count on his support and help.

He was the best guy to put Marcos on the right path. He would be able to listen to Marcos and understand him, but also guide him without making any compromises. Their collaboration proved to be fruitful. In 2002, when he was seventeen, Marcos reached his first junior Grand Slam final and pulled himself up to No. 2 in the ITF world junior rankings behind Richard Gasquet.

I remained very close to "my" young Cypriot. He let me know of any doubts he was having and relied on me whenever he had to make an important decision. After he parted company with Jean-Paul, Marcos told me again that I was the one who knew him the best and in whom he had the greatest confidence.

When he split with Guillaume Peyre, his second trainer, at the end of 2004, after a two years collaboration together, he asked me to take charge of him.

By then, I was already a professional coach. He had seen me develop with Irena, whom he had known for five years and the results spoke for themselves. Not wanting to take me away from her, he asked if I could be in charge of his training while continuing to work with Irena. I accepted without hesitation.

I was therefore coaching those two players side by side, but it was to the detriment of Irena. Marcos occupied a lot of my time and I wasn't there for Irena as much as I had been. Eventually I suggested to her that she should work with another coach at the academy. My Cypriot was rapidly producing miracles. Having gone back down to around No.

250 in the world rankings, he then made very quick progress. He won some Challenger events and then played in his first big tournament at Bratislava in Slovakia. He came through qualifying and then fought through to the final to play the local favourite, Dominik Hrbaty, who was world No. 14 at the time. Marcos beat him (7–6 7–6) despite the gap of 236 places in the world rankings! And on Hrbaty's home soil!

Marcos has always needed rankings goals to motivate himself. After that win in Bratislava we decided that 2005 would be the year he would break into the world's top 50. That seemed achievable. Marcos was euphoric and surpassed himself. He always seemed to be surprised by his results. Every time he put in a really good performance he would say to me, with his eyes open wide and with a big smile on his face: "Patrick, how about that?"

At the end of January, after the year had barely started, he had already reached his goal by getting to the last 16 of the Australian Open after squeezing through the qualifying tournament. Unfortunately relationship problems with his long-term girlfriend tarnished the joy of his victories. Marcos thought deeply about things and sank into a form of depression. The second fly in the ointment was that I wasn't travelling with him when he played abroad. My children were very young and I could not accept seeing them only fifteen weeks of the year. My absence hit him hard and served only to reinforce his sense of abandonment, which he had already been feeling when his parents sent him to live in Paris without them and against his wishes.

His depression deepened over the months. He complained that his life was devoid of interest, friends or pleasure.

His despair followed him around all day along. His shoulders were hunched, his head hung low and he totally lost his smile. Tennis itself has never been an objective for Marcos. He threw himself into it so that his father would be proud of him, but their relationship had gone seriously downhill.

I was not up to the job at that time. My affection for him was too strong and I neglected my role as a coach. It shocked me that this young lad from a modest background, who at the age of nineteen was already in the world's top 50 and was on the brink of a promising career, was feeling sorry for himself all day long. He had achieved what I had dreamed of doing and I could not understand his disinterest. A coach would not have made a judgement and would instead have simply looked for solutions. I did not act as I should have done. His depression touched me on a personal level. I tried to shake him out of it, but clearly to no effect.

With everything else failing, I decided in September 2005, just after the US Open, to sting him into a reaction. I sat opposite him and talked to him man to man: "Marcos, you don't have a right to feel sorry for yourself and to give up your work. Your parents sacrificed their family life for you. Your mother accepted losing you when you were only thirteen so that you would have the opportunity to live this adventure. As for me, I've invested a lot of money in you over the last seven years. You don't have the right to let everyone down now. Believe me, it's in your interests to get on with it." I was hard and cold. I talked to him about money whereas he needed to hear about feelings. We were on completely different wavelengths.

Today I understand what he felt at that moment. He said to himself that I had never loved him and that everything I had done had been for financial reasons. He saw my refusal to travel with him as an abdication of my responsibilities, as a disenchantment – while he only understood messages of love. His ultra-sensibility was both his strength and his weakness.

This episode gave Marcos the chance to pull himself together, to get back to work like a maniac and to reach the final of the Australian Open five months later. But that conversation also brought about our eventual parting, because it generated a feeling of betrayal, which our relationship would not survive. When I spoke to him I knew that I was taking a big risk but I could not come up with any other method to provoke a reaction in him.

At the same time I did not imagine that the crisis,

which was to follow would sound the death knell for our relationship. In my mind a father and a son love each other until they die and the love within them enables them to overcome all crises. That was how I saw things, but he did not look at them in the same way.

From the day we ended our collaboration onwards, Marcos went back to his work like a madman. He worked harder than he had ever done before. He put together a spectacular number of training sessions with maximum intensity. He quickly crowned his efforts by reaching a final at Basel in October, two months after. He had dropped back down the rankings but this result enabled him to finish the year around No. 50 in the world. However, he was ready to aim much higher. I asked Guillaume Peyre to take charge of him again and to travel with him. My own situation with Marcos was ambiguous. I had to stay in contact because I gave the motivation he needed to work hard, but I also had to give him some space because he was in the process of breaking free; he loved me and hated me at the same time.

The tournament circuit started up again in January 2006. He reached the quarter-finals at Doha in Qatar and lost to Federer. He was extremely disappointed. He was in tears when he called me, overwhelmed by this defeat against one of the great athletes in history who at the time was the undisputed king of world tennis. Then he told me:

"Patrick, if I win the Australian Open I'll be in the top 10." He was in the zone. I knew it. I felt it. He believed what he was saying. I encouraged him, sensing that he was not far away from being able to achieve this. What self-assurance! I love that. It's for moments like that, that I do this job.

The Australian Open, the first Grand slam tournament of the year, started and Marcos reeled off some big wins: he knocked out Stepanek and Roddick and then beat Ljubicic in the quarter-finals. Many of the matches went to five sets, but he won each of these marathons, thanks to his faultless physical preparation. The hours which he had spent on the court giving 100 per cent were starting to pay off. Watching him on TV everyday, I wasn't sleeping any more. The matches were at night and I obviously watched all of them. I would talk on the phone to Marcos and to Guillaume. It was decided that I would get on a plane immediately after he won his quarter-final. I threw some things into a case and dashed to the airport. Forty-eight hours later I was in the stadium to witness a story-book semi-final against David Nalbandian which Marcos won 6–4 in the final set. I was exultant. Journalists from around the world wanted to know where this charismatic twenty-one-year-old player had come from to stage the hold–up of the century and drop like a bomb into the world of tennis at the highest level.

I did a series of interviews and improvised press

conferences. In the end Marcos lost in the final to Roger Federer, the master (who that day won the seventh of his 17 Grand Slam titles), but only after having shaken him by going a set and a break up and then having a point for a double break before losing in four sets.

For the first time my Academy was in the spotlight. Marcos played the game. When he spoke after the match he paid a vibrant homage to the structure which had welcomed him six years earlier and had enabled him to realise his talent. I received hundreds of text messages. In a flash I was no longer anonymous.

However, I kept a cool head. What Marcos had achieved was great, but it was only a beginning. The road was still long. He had pulled off a feat, but he had still to reach the world's top 10, which he was now close to doing and he still had to show that he had it in him to become a Grand Slam champion. Unfortunately, that was not what Marcos heard. One week later we were talking at the academy and what I heard did not please me at all: "I now know how to play to get to the top. I don't want to work as hard any more. I know myself. If I carry on like this I will burn myself out, I will lose my desire and I won't be effective in matches."

"Marcos, we both know how you have got to this point..."

"I've told you that I understand that. I'm the one

who has done it and I'm the one who knows."

For the moment I was not insistent. I thought it was a case of post-tournament decompression. I knew what immense efforts he had made to lift himself out of his state of depression and the amount of work he had put in.

The results that followed were obviously disappointing. He was missing the boat. He needed to ride the wave of his confidence and in order to do that it was imperative that he did not slacken off. I talked to Guillaume, but he could not make Marcos see reason.

He still reached the Wimbledon semi-finals that year, lifted by the environment and favoured by a playing surface that was ideal for him, but the rest of his results were not good. I was faced with a question of conscience. I had immense affection for him, but our relationship had to remain professional. His father often called me: "Marcos cannot carry on like this. You have to make him react. Kick him out of the academy. He needs an electric shock. Do it for me, in the name of our friendship." Christos was using a form of emotional blackmail on me. I knew that Marcos needed to be taken into hand and that I was the only person who could do that, but I didn't want to send him away from the academy for fear that it would be the end for him. At the time I did not understand him, but in reality he unwittingly felt that with this result he had largely repaid all his debts to everyone. Tennis had never been his choice. He had sacrificed everything – his life in Cyprus, his family, his friends. His parents, the Benhaim family, me, everyone who mattered to him – they could all feel proud. The little Cypriot had reached the final of a Grand Slam tournament and was ranked in the world's top 10. We were even. He was empty, exhausted by the years he had spent fighting. He had not even been able to enjoy this status that he had fought so hard to acquire. His existential questions came back like an old refrain.

At Indian Wells in March 2007, after another early defeat in the tournament, I decided to intervene again: "Marcos, you must do something. You must go back to work."

"No. You haven't been in a Grand Slam final. I have. I know what I need to do to start again. Believe in me."

"You've also achieved that thanks to a strategy that has been put in place for you for several years. You're telling me, at the very moment when you are reaping the rewards of your work, that you must make radical changes. That doesn't make sense.

"I know myself. I know what I need to do."

"And I know where that is going to lead you. You're in the process of climbing into a boat which is going to sink and you're asking me to climb on board with you. If that's your choice, do as you like, but it will be without me."

"Are you threatening me?"

"No, it's not a threat. I have a responsibility. I refuse to see you head for disaster while I just stand there with my arms crossed. The scenario has been laid out. I've already waited a long time; in this sport you can't make up for lost time."

"You can't make me do that. You can't expel me from the academy. It's my family."

"Your parents are your family. I love you a lot, but I have a professional responsibility for you. Your parents confided you to my care so that I could achieve an objective. You think you're in the right, but you're wrong. You think you know, but you don't. I want to go to the very top. If you want to come with me you are welcome. We will go together. If you want to take another route that's your decision. But in that case allow me the right not to go along with you."

He was in tears. Marcos had the impression that I was taking away my affection and my trust. I was in a corner. His results continued to be unworthy of a player of his level. He turned up for matches ill–prepared. In those conditions it's difficult to feel strong.

Although I had not reached the point of deciding to expel him from the academy, his father called him just before Wimbledon in 2007 and told him that I had decided to do just that – and that I was getting ready to tell him this. Marcos turned up at the house that we rented during the tournament and told me he was leaving. I felt wounded. What betrayal on the part of Christos! I won't deny it. I wanted Marcos to keep his relationship with his father, despite how turbulent it was. At the same time I was furious with him. I called him as soon as Marcos left: "Christos, how could you do that? You lied to Marcos. That was a scandalous way to go about things."

"You've done nothing for a year! I asked you several times to kick him out. I had to do something."

"You betrayed me and that is unacceptable. I will not forgive you for that."

It would be our last conversation. A few months later I stood back far enough to assess what had happened. I had been a wretched coach. Marcos had certainly achieved things with us, by becoming world junior champion in 2003, then by reaching a Grand Slam final three years later and finally breaking into the world's top 10, but I hadn't known how to handle him. Worse still, I had cut myself off from him. Our relationship was at the heart of the problem. The attachment was too strong. It was because I had been unable to stand back from the situation that I was so ineffective. I didn't behave like a coach.

My emotions had got the better of me and I had criticised his decisions rather than find the way to make him make better choices. I was sad to lose my spiritual son because I was very attached to him. In reality I lost out on both counts, personally and professionally. It was a good lesson for me to learn. In the future I would keep a strong affection for my players but I would still retain the capacity to stand back, which is indispensable in the job of coaching. I would no longer let my feelings get in the way of my professional choices. In addition, I had not achieved my objective. I wanted to be the best and I had failed. I had lost this battle, but I would use it to win those that lay ahead.

8
On the tour

*"Football starts with the head, continues
through the heart and ends up in the feet."*
Jose Mourinho

With Marcos out of my life, I decided to follow my own path. I learned a lesson: always look at things objectively. Be totally involved, but at the same time keep the necessary distance to keep a cool head. I would never again let myself get sidetracked by these awful emotions that had made me lose sight of my goal.

I decided to concentrate again on Irena, who was not making the progress I had wanted. She had stagnated around number 500 in the world rankings, which was where I had left her a year earlier. It was time for her to come out of her lair and show what she was capable of. She had worked with several coaches during my absence but hadn't believed in any of them enough to blossom and progress. She was enthusiastic about my return and

I started to coach her again.

My first objective was obvious: to make he competitive in matches. Over the years she had developed an annoying tendency to give up the fight when in trouble. It's a phenomenon you often see in tennis players today. Many players just don't hang on in there when the score is going against them. I wanted to know what was going on inside her head. I needed to put my finger on what was making her switch off in a match and accept defeat while everything was still to play for.

I have learned to make a distinction between the behaviour of a player and what is their true nature. Behaviour is simply what you do in reaction to something. In a given situation, the reaction is automatic. Even if the player is not getting the desired result, he or she will systematically reproduce this behaviour in a parallel situation. In a certain set of circumstances, he will delve into his personal box of tools but will be helpless because he just does not have the right tool at his disposal. In a situation where emotions are running too high, he is blinded and automatically picks a tool that is inadequate for the job in hand. This reflex then generates beliefs which lock him into a vicious circle. But these conditioned reactions do not define the person. All you need to do is "reprogramme" him.

I wasn't looking to change Irena's character. I just wanted to change certain things that she did, in order to help her to reach her goals. I had to tackle the problem at the root, to understand the internal battles that were going on inside her. She had lost so many matches in the past that when she found herself in a difficult situation she was convinced that things would end in the same unfortunate way. She hated the thought of this and preferred simply to give up the fight; she was like someone driving a car into a wall and shutting their eyes. Accepting defeat, especially without putting up a fight, was a less painful outcome. That gives a glimpse of an alternative: "If I had fought, I might have won…"

It's important to understand that a player who "tanks" like that goes through a lot of suffering. They leave the court having endured two defeats. They have lost both the match and his pride. They feel weak and ugly. In losing without putting up a fight, Irena was destroying herself. I understood her suffering and decided to join forces with her and support her.

One day she played a match in practice against a player who had come to the academy for a trial. She was a promising young player whom I was very keen to recruit. As happened all too often, Irena found herself 4-1 down in the first set and then threw in the towel. She allowed herself to be flattened all too quickly in two sets.   Anyone who watched and knows a bit about tennis would have said that her attitude was unacceptable. It's important to understand what a coach feels when confronted with this kind of situation. He feels publicly humiliated by his player's offhand manner and lack of respect. Despite all the efforts that we have both made previously, the player does not even try to win!

In general a competitor who "tanks" does not keep the same coach for long. The coach's frustration is too great. He sees the situation as a total lack of respect for him and for his work, which ends the relationship between the teacher and his student. In my case it was even worse. She had humiliated not only her coach but also the head of the academy – and had done so in front of a player who was thinking of joining my organisation. I had to accept this behaviour while keeping my mouth shut! I saw this match as a very difficult test mentally. That was without taking into consideration the fact that the opportunity to recruit the young player had been thrown into serious doubt...

I left the court and gave myself a few moments on my own for reflection. I knew that if I followed my emotions nothing good would come of it. I had to distance myself in order to react in a professional fashion. I had to put my experience with Marcos to good use. The man in me had been affected on a moral level, but it had to be the coach who reacted. There should be only one objective: to ensure that this bad experience did not happen again. I had to turn the situation to my advantage, to profit from this stumble and come out as a winner.

Having thought it through for ten minutes, I came up with an idea. I went back to the academy clubhouse to look for Irena. A moment later I was in my office sitting opposite her. I asked her to give me her debrief on the match. She looked at the floor, blushing with shame: "I played very badly. I'm disappointed. Nothing went right today."

"Did she give you tactical problems?"

"No, it was just me. I couldn't keep the ball in the court."

"I agree, Irena. You played a bad match. But the only person responsible for that is me. I didn't prepare you properly."

"…"

"Neither you nor I want that to happen again, do we?"

"No, of course we don't!"

"Then you have to help me to improve. You and me, we want the same thing. If you help me, we will get there."

"How?"

"It's simple. You must talk to me. You must have been particularly tense before today's match. That's part of life in sport. It's not a problem. But if I don't know what you're feeling inside I can't help you. I could have reassured you. I could have prepared you better mentally. I didn't do that. You must tell me these things and then we'll react accordingly, together, so that this doesn't happen agai

She lifted up her head and gave incredulous look.

"It's unbelievable ! I thought you were going to kill me."

"Why would I have done that? It wasn't your fault. It was mine."

I had won. In this type of situation she had grown accustomed to being given a severe ticking-off. I had broken the cycle. We were working together. I was in the same camp as her and we were going to win this war. That day, thanks to a solid relationship built on trust, she felt that someone had backed her up. It was a trigger that would make her become stronger.

Results were not slow in coming. She quickly climbed towards the top 300 in the world rankings until a sprain forced her to take a break for five weeks.

I branched out in order to continue my own progress. I started to work in parallel with a twenty-four-year-old Ukrainian player, Julia Vakulenko, who was ranked around No. 120 in the world. My methods were working, because the players were making progress. While Irena was climbing up the ladder, Julia had made an enormous leap in the rankings and had risen to No. 33 in the world, beating Mauresmo and Clijsters along the way.

Constantly switching between the two players

vas very enriching for me, because their psychological profiles were completely different. I had to adapt. My attitude towards each of them and the way I spoke to them was completely different. With one of them I had to be hard and extremely demanding; with the other I had to be attentive, tuned-in and understanding.

> *"You need only one night to learn how to box.*
> *To learn how to fight you need a whole life."*
> Alessandro Baricco

When Irena started training again I decided to go with her to her first tournament to help her get back into the swing of things. It was a big Challenger tournament in the US, with prize money of $100,000 on offer.

She took part in the qualifying competition as her ranking was not high enough to get her into the main draw. She won her first match against a player ranked in the world's top 300, which was a fine win considering that she was coming back from injury. But in the second round, even though she was facing a player ranked considerably lower than her, Irena could not break loose. She was so tense that the ball just did not come off her racket. Despite her efforts she was soon trailing 6–3, 5–2. When she went back to her chair at the changeover I felt I could not just settle for her losing the match.

From my seat I whispered to her: "Irena, we're

going to win this match. We're going to play each point together, one after another."

I then moved behind the wire netting on her side of the court so that I could encourage her and give her some tactical guidance after every point. She forced herself to make a huge effort and as a result kept the match alive. She finally won the second set 7–5 by winning five games in a row. The third set was tight right till the end but she ended it by winning the tie-break. It was an immense psychological victory. Irena had pushed herself to her very limits.

The next day, when she was due to play in the last round of the qualifying competition, she met in the hotel a young player from New Zealand who, like her, had Serbian roots. She was playing in the main draw by dint of her world ranking. Her name: Marina Erakovic. Irena had huge admiration for her. Having played her in the juniors, she remembered smarting defeats that had been inflicted on her by a player of high quality. They chatted in Serbian for ten minutes.

When Irena rejoined me I asked her: "Did you tell her that you were going to win your last qualifying match today and then beat her in the first round of the main draw?" Irena laughed, but her face lit up with pride. She felt that I believed in her, that I respected her level more than I did for the other player.

The next day my player lost in the final round of

qualifying. Mentally she was empty. The fight she had put up the day before had required enormous energy and after it she had totally eased off. A win like that should have given her a boost, but she was still struggling to maintain her effort over a long period when under pressure.

We returned to the hotel after her defeat. In the evening my phone rang. It was the tournament referee, who told me that a player in the main draw had pulled out and that Irena's name had been drawn out of the hat to replace her. She would play in the first round the next day... against Marina Erakovic. What fantastic news. I was jubilant. I immediately ran out of my room to go and tell Irena. When she opened the door of her room and learned what had happened, she stood there open-mouthed. Her eyes staring open wide, she was unable to utter a word. She stood on the doorstep of her room, speechless, her arms dangling down, her mouth half-open. I said to her straight away that we must meet for dinner. I had only one evening in which to prepare her for victory.

The previous day's match felt like a premonition. It would be essential in terms of getting her to understand how well she was playing, which was something of which she was not yet aware. If she were to win, she would conclude that the progress she had made had put her ahead of this other player she so admired. She would have made a big mental breakthrough. I had a tactical plan in mind and I had to convince Irena that if she followed it she would win.

I was proved right. Irena won 6–4, 6–4 by playing a solid and controlled match from start to finish. She immediately called her father to tell him. He also had great respect for Erakovic. For him, Erakovic was a model top-level player, who would always beat his daughter.

Irena came back to me after she had spoken to him. She was aggrieved: "Listen to this! He didn't believe that I had beaten her! It's crazy!" This story showed how much he had lost faith in Irena. With his view coloured by several years of defeats, he under-estimated his daughter's level in relation to other players. Without being aware of it, he had dragged down her confidence and made her doubt herself. She was cut in two: she carried the weight of her past and she dreamed of the future. Her father had done remarkable work with her over a period of many years, giving her a powerful game and extraordinary ball-striking ability. He had built the player she was today. But the doubt that he had unconsciously instilled in her had weakened her and made her fearful. At this stage of her career my contribution was vital for her.

Irena beat another player ranked in the top 150 of the world before losing to Yung–Jan Chan, the world No. 50. She lost 6–4 in the third set after a bitter fight. Her season had taken off. I had done my job and I could return to Paris.

Just before Roland Garros, the world junior No. 1, Anastasia Pavlyuchenkova, came to the academy to work there with her coaching team, which comprised her father and her brother. At the start of the tournament she asked me to come to her matches. She lost in the semi-finals of the junior competition.

Three weeks later, at Wimbledon, she was given a wild card into the main draw of the women's singles but was beaten 6-0, 6-0 by Hantuchova. I was there with Julia Vakulenko. Anastasia asked to see me. "For six months I haven't been going anywhere. I'm going to compete in the Wimbledon junior tournament [which takes place during the second week of the senior event] and I really need your help. Would you be able to prepare me for the tournament?"

Thus I set out on another adventure.

> *"A problem without a solution*
> *is a poorly stated problem."*
> Albert Einstein

When I started working with Nastia (as she is known) it was in a loaded atmosphere. I remember seeing all four of the family (father, mother, brother and her) sitting at a table in the tournament restaurant. They were sitting there with their heads bowed, not engaging in any conversation whatsoever. Their relationships were extremely tense and the young Russian herself was petrified. In practice she was tight and her legs moved very slowly. Six empty months in terms of results combined with the psychological shock of this terrible defeat at Wimbledon had seriously undermined her essential confidence.

She had finished 2006 as the world junior champion but now she could barely win a match at this level. Among the pros she had stagnated at around No. 300 for six months. She lost as early as the quarter–finals in the Wimbledon junior event and did not make any progress in the months that followed. Her father, who was always at her practices, did not understand her poor results or why his daughter did not take notice of what he said to her. As a result he was permanently dragging her down by making offensive and negative comments about her game. He was suffering and could not keep a lid on his emotions. Every practice session took place in an atmosphere of stress and aggression. Her father shouted at her in Russian. She screamed back at him, she panicked and she threw her racket... She was going out on the court with no aim in mind. She was just hoping that by some miracle she would play better, feel better and rediscover in herself the confidence which she was so lacking. Obviously, the opposite happened. There was no miracle. Disillusionment replaced hope and she fell apart.

On a purely technical level I was surprised by how poor she was. Her ball-striking was all wrong and her timing was off. In competition she just allowed her opponents to dictate all the points. Every match was an ordeal, whoever the opponent was. However hard she fought on any point, at no time did she give the impression that she was on top of her opponent.

Despite what was happening I tried to keep a cool head. Off the court Nastia talked to me a lot and would systematically run herself down: "I've got nothing mentally" or "I'm stupid". My contribution had to be just right. Despite the difficult time she was going through, she showed some dignity. She assured me that it was all her fault and that what I was doing was very good. For a girl of seventeen, she impressed me with her courage and the way she took on responsibility.

For the moment I was taking her practice sessions, but I hadn't decided on the best way to proceed. Before defining my strategy I would need to make sure that everything was in place. When a coach begins to choose his options and to point the way ahead, he must do so with absolute commitment. He cannot "try" to go in a certain direction; instead he must go for it with determination and bring his player along with him. You must go about things with certainty rather than with conjecture. You will not make progress if you are dealing in suppositions.

For the moment we had to get our heads down, let the storm blow over and even use it to our advantage. These extreme moments are actually interesting because they reveal much about the player. It's in situations of great difficulty or of great success that character traits emerge with the most force and clarity. It was the time when I could discover things that would help me later to understand my player's situation and how she functioned.

In this sort of situation many coaches would be tempted to concentrate on making technical improvements. It's a reassuring approach because they are dealing with the subject that they know best. But it was not a trap that I was going to fall into. I had to focus on her.

My aim was not to give myself reassurance, but to get her out of this bad situation. There was no way that she would have achieved what she had if she'd had these technical deficiencies in the past. It was obvious that the stress she was suffering every day had affected her technique. Improvement in her game would come through rediscovering her serenity in practice and in competition.

I saw a player who was afraid, who did not want to fail, who hoped that her opponent would make the fatal mistake before she did. Her outlook on tennis at that time meant that she was playing on her back foot. Her fear of failure slowed her movement down and as a result she was making contact with the ball too far back. She positioned herself too deep in the court. If I questioned her technique now, at a time when she had such doubts, I would only risk adding to her suffering.

In September 2007 Julia Vakulenko reached the highest ranking position of her career. When she made the last 16 of the US Open we parted company. I did not see things in the same way as one of those close to her and I refused to go along with his methods. I gave her a choice: me or him. She chose him, citing the fact that he had been with her for eight years.

Julia went on to tumble down the rankings and ended up retiring two years later. I was hurt and surprised by her choice. She had made real progress with me, which was evident in her huge jump in the rankings, which she had never made in the past. How could she choose this weird individual she was close to when she had been going nowhere with him for years?

It was vital that I found an answer to this question. Perhaps she was unaware of the progress she had made with me? Perhaps the person she had chosen reassured her more than I could and thereby offered her more hope for the future than I could guarantee her? Whatever the answer, I wasn't satisfied by the outcome: we were to stop working together at the very time when she had made her biggest ever jump in the world rankings.

At the end of 2007 Irena climbed into the top 300

on the WTA rankings list. She had passed a real milestone, but going forward she would need someone to travel with her to tournaments. A coach from my academy would now work with her full–time.

After the good results that Irena had achieved, I then concentrated on Nastia, who at the end of the year was still struggling. The months that followed showed a small improvement, but she continued to travel with her parents, without me and I knew that the ambiance wasn't right for her development.

Just like Irena, her father had done some great work with her. Starting out again with a blank sheet, he had turned her into the best junior in the world. After that, unfortunately, a run of bad results left her father uncontrollably stressed, which affected her behaviour.

At the Australian Open in January 2008 her parents asked to see me. They wanted me to work full-time with her and travel with her. They told me that I was the best person for this job and promised to give me their full confidence and support. I talked things over with my wife and then agreed to travel with Nastia to a set number of tournaments which we agreed in advance. However, I did not agree to work only with Nastia. I wanted to be able to continue working with other players. We therefore agreed that she would share me with other players while she was competing in tournaments. From my side I wanted to carry on learning and was convinced that having a range of experiences would enable me to develop the most quickly.

> *"Knowledge is acquired by experience; everything else is just information."*
>
> Anonymous

In March 2008 Yung–Jan Chan, a Taiwanese player, sought my help. She was No. 50 in singles in the WTA rankings and top 10 in doubles. I agreed to give her some help, notably at Indian Wells and Miami, because she had never won a single match at tournaments of that importance.

We embarked on a period of intensive preparation ahead of this American swing and it was agreed that I would accompany her there. She reached the last 16 in California before losing to Davenport 6-4 in the third set. It was a good result, though it left a bitter taste in my mouth because she could have won the match.

In Miami she lost to Kuznetsova in three sets in the second round. With the support of her parents, she asked me to carry on working with her, full-time. When I said no, they were insistent: "Just name your price. We absolutely want you to continue coaching her. We can already see some big changes in her." However, it was not a question of money; I wanted to remain free. I was supporting

Aravane Rezai at a number of tournaments at the request of her father, I was working with Irena when she came back to Paris between tournaments, and of course I had a commitment with Nastia; at that stage I was not yet ready to be tied to a single player, no matter how promising she was.

But Yung–Jan stuck to her guns. At one coaching session she took me to one side: "I need you. I have a lot of ranking points to defend between now and June. My qualification for the Olympic Games in Beijing is at stake. It's essential for me to qualify, because if I don't I will lose all my contracts." I agreed to devote my time to her for two months, to enable her to get over this tricky hurdle. She eventually went on to book her place at the Olympics and won the doubles title in Rome, which was one of her greatest successes.

"To talk is a necessity; to listen is an art."
Goethe

At Roland Garros I concentrated on Nastia again, Yung–Jan Chan having agreed to work with another coach from the academy. In the intervening period I got to know the young Russian well. I knew how I needed to deal with her in the future. I eventually drew up a strategy.

My plan of action was based on two simple concepts that enable a player to win in competition: stress and confidence.

Stress is necessary. It is the essence of competition. Without stress, you cannot perform. However, it must be balanced by confidence, or it can be counter-productive. Stress and confidence exist alongside each other in an unstable equilibrium which can change at any moment. However, it is this equilibrium that guarantees the quality of performance in competition. There are many ways in which you can raise confidence levels. There are equally many ways in which you can raise or lower the levels of stress. I would have to juggle these parameters to help Nastia recover her efficiency on the court.

To this effect I put in place a plan of action in four interlocking stages:

Find the ideal method of communication.

Improve her efficiency in matches.

Find ways of compensating for her poor movement.

Improve her positioning on the court
(In the mid–term).

1. Find the ideal method of communication
A coach's job is to impart and in order to do that he must create a favourable environment. Too many teachers are wells of knowledge but fall down

through their lack of teaching skills. It is better to have a simple message and to put it across perfectly than to have an enormous quantity of information which you are unable to convey. For a coach to be effective he needs his player's total confidence above anything else.

My father always used to say to me: "Power doesn't come to you, it needs to be taken." However, beware: force is not the only way of taking power and it's certainly not the best way. If I want to have an effect on the player I am coaching, the player must have total confidence in me. There is no miracle formula for this, though there are number of methods to be recommended that can be useful.

Listen rather than talk
Every player has a head full of opinions about their own game, about their strengths, about their weaknesses, about what is right for them and what is not. The coach needs to be aware of these opinions and to take them into account. When a coach talks before listening, there is a good chance he will find himself contradicting certain strong beliefs held by the player. He will then find himself at odds with the player.

Besides, the less you speak the more weight your words will carry. Every stance the coach takes has a very important impact if he does not misuse it.

By listening rather than talking, by endeavouring

to engage in dialogue, you develop the ability to understand one another. In taking an interest in your player's cultural and family history, you get inside his head, you enter his world. You need to forget yourself, forget your own values and your own culture in order to enter a different world.

Besides, we have available a goldmine of information which needs to be observed, heard and understood before it can be put to use. I am constantly seeking to observe. I notice every detail: people's choice of clothes, how they look, whether they are well turned out, their hair, whether they are close-shaved or not: if they are not, is their new beard trimmed? How they interact with other people: what is their tone of voice when talking to others? What words do they use? What do you read into the way they behave in the company of different people? How do they react in each situation? What emotions do you see in them in response to certain things that are said, certain situations, certain attitudes of other people towards them or towards a third party?

Many opportunities are presented to us to collect information which could be vital at any given moment. A blink of the eye, a slight reddening of the cheeks, a raised eyebrow or even just the tone of my player's response – they are all indications of which I take heed and which inform me about the way they are feeling, what is going on inside them. In the evening my mind ponders all these pieces of information and goes back over them, to the extent that I am eventually so in sync with my player that I know what they are feeling in every situation in life, I know what words generate what emotions in him. I can then gauge, at any moment, their mental state and know what to say to them to influence them one way or the other. Little by little, I get to a point where I can hear what they are thinking rather than what that are saying.

Gain the respect of the player and don't lose it

There are strong and universal values associated with sport such as integrity, work, perseverance, calmness and reflection. In embodying those values I am taking up a role in my relationship with my player. In his work, "The Pacific Warrior", Dan Millman wisely advises: "Embody what you teach and only teach what you embody."

In order to maintain the authority which is indispensable when you are teaching, you must never find yourself in a situation where you are having to plead your own case. That is the mistake that many parents make. When they feel obliged to justify themselves, they are putting themselves on the same level as the child. The child's reference points are consequently turned upside down and as a result the parents find it increasingly difficult to command respect.

It is imperative to show your maturity in your everyday behaviour when you take decisions in difficult situations. You must always remain in control of your emotions.

Be on your player's side
If the player feels you are with them, that they are your whole focus, that you are making their objectives your own, that you have at your disposal solutions which will help them achieve those goals, they will be much more inclined to listen to you and do as you say. If, moreover, you never judge them and instead guide them, if you take on board their mistakes and their failures, they will come to have great confidence in you.

Adapt to your student's means of communication
When you make a decision, do it in a way that brooks no argument.

Certain players require freedom, others need a firm hand, others blossom only under absolute authority. Some react badly to criticism, no matter how constructive it might be, others only get the best out of themselves when they are constantly called into question.

Nothing is set in stone. The expression "the weather's nice" means different things in Marseille and in Paris. The term "motivation" does not have the same significance for everyone. It's essential that you adapt what you say according to the personality of the player you're working with. If you don't, they might not understand your message.

You can't convince someone when you're standing outside their door. In our job we need to be invited in. For that to happen we must talk the same language as the student, so that we are both on the same page.

I had reached this position of strength with Nastia. She was convinced that I was the right man at the right time, the one who could get her out of this tight corner. I had won her trust and her confidence. She listened to me. From now onwards I knew how to talk to her and what to do with her.

From a young age Nastia had been handled with a rod of iron. I had to continue with this approach so that I did not break with her father's style of coaching.

I decided therefore that I would be firm with her, but at the same time positive and encouraging. With every word I would make her appreciate my belief in her and my admiration for her.

2. Improve her efficiency in matches.
Her stress levels were too high and were paralysing her in competition. Her expectations were such that the idea of not playing well destroyed her efficiency. Therefore one of the first things I did was adapt what I said to her, so that she looked at things in the mid-term rather than the short-term. I gave her goals in matches to build her game with the aim of developing weapons for the months ahead. I

wanted to disconnect her from the short term and from her expectations, which were causing her too much stress.

When I briefed her before each match I always underlined this point. I told her that the result did not matter, but at the same time the goals which I set her in terms of her game had to be respected. In my heart I knew that if she did respect them she would see the result in the short term – but I made sure I did not tell her that. In truth, winning matches was my main objective, because I knew that they would help to keep in check the stress that was handicapping her.

3. Compensate for her poor movement on court

It is difficult to win a match when you are not moving well. For the moment Nastia's movement was failing her. In the short term the only possible option was to avoid her having to cover much of the court. It was crucial that my player was always the first one to attack, to never let herself be dominated, but to dictate. I therefore focused my efforts on her serve and her returns. The way she started a point was vital: if she was the first to attack she would at best be able to win the point or, at worst, she would dictate the point and make her opponent run.

*4. Improve her positioning on the court
(In the mid–term).*

With my physical trainer, we put in place a plan of action to ensure that Nastia would make progress in this area.

I also undertook to ensure that she lost some weight. Excess weight is a tennis player's number one enemy. This is a sport which demands speed and the ability to change direction as quickly as possible. Try to play with a heavy bag on your back and you will understand this. Nastia needed to lose eight kilos. I put her on a diet which I went on too in a show of solidarity. Over the space of a few months she made the desired weight loss, as did I.

Results were not slow in coming. At Roland-Garros Nastia qualified for the main draw before losing to Flavia Pennetta. She was making progress. Her confidence was coming back.

At Wimbledon she made another breakthrough. After qualifying she beat Li Na and Alizé Cornet and lost only in the third round. She was not far off making the top 100, but went through a dip in the summer: she became less aggressive and started to let opponents dominate her again. As she was more often on the defensive, her efficiency dipped. But I wasn't going to give up on anything. There was no question about it: we would continue to progress. My job was to find solutions. When we were flying back on the plane from Tokyo, at the end of the Asian swing, I decided on electric shock treatment. I went back over all the matches she had played that year and asked her to give me a mark for her level of aggression in each one. The results told their own story: "You lost every one of the matches where you marked your level of aggression below five out of ten. On the other hand you won every single match where you marked it above eight out of ten. The conclusion is obvious. To win, there is only one way to play. More than that, you must appreciate that you will be making progress in every match in which you are playing aggressively. When you play in a defensive and fearful frame of mind, you are going backwards." That conversation triggered something in her mind.

At the end of the year she went on an unbelievable run, winning two $100,000 tournaments in a row. She broke into the top 50. Four months later she reached the semi-finals at Indian Wells, beating Jankovic and Radwanska, two top five players, along the way.

The quarter–final against Radwanska threw up an interesting coaching story. In the second set Nastia let herself think too much about impending victory and her aggressiveness dipped. She held her serve, but could not break her opponent's. She was hitting her returns from well behind the baseline, which meant she could not take advantage of the weakness of her opponent's second serves.

At WTA tournaments players can call their coach

on to the court once in each set at a change of ends. She asked for me to come on the court when she was leading 4-3. I came on with the intention of telling her to position herself inside the baseline so that she could attack her opponent on both her first and second serves. But as I approached I could see fear and panic in her face. In a flash I decided to change my instructions.   Telling her to play more aggressively would only feed her fear, because she would view that as taking risks. When fear grips us, the last thing we want to do is to take risks. I therefore changed tack and decided to send her in the opposite direction to what sporting logic told me. I had thirty seconds in which to bring her the maximum serenity. "You're taking too many chances on your opponent's serves. It's not necessary. She is slow getting into the point and isn't putting you in any sort of difficulty. Stay behind the baseline and start each point slowly. That won't hurt you." A game of poker.

I returned to my seat, curious to find out what reaction my intervention would produce. Radwanska served, Nastia stepped a metre into the court and cracked a return winner. From 0-15 it went to 0-30, 0-40 and a break to love, My player went on to serve for the match and won with authority.

When I think back on it, I realise with amusement that I told her to do the opposite of what was required, and that from her side she did the opposite of what I had told her… for the better.

In the end, by influencing her emotional state I had created a situation in which she could take risks. The little time that I had been given, had not given me the option of going into technical or tactical matters. I had therefore concentrated on working on her emotional state, which was not helping her to play well, and it had worked.

Nastia, who had been around the 300 mark in the world rankings a year earlier, was now up to No. 27. A whole new path was opening up for her. Her progress in all areas was there to see with every passing tournament. She was playing the sort of tennis which made her more efficient. The paralysed young player had been replaced by one who was charging ahead like a steamroller.

"If people don't listen, let adversity teach them."
Ethiopian proverb

However, this was the moment that Nastia chose to call everything into question.
A month after Indian Wells we were in Madrid. The young Russian was preparing to play her first match, against Shuai Peng. During dinner she was in top form.

Suddenly she interrupted me and said in a serious voice: "I want to tell you that I don't agree with the way you make me play. My game style has always been different. I'm an intelligent player on court, a strategist. I became world junior number one by playing that type of tennis. You make me hit every ball aggressively and that doesn't suit me. I think you don't understand my game."

She was clearly awaiting a response from me, but the injustice of what she had said had left me speechless. In the space of a year, which had started with her floundering, her career had taken off in spectacular fashion. The previous year she had won the award for the player who had made the most progress up the world rankings. She was casting doubt on my work when I had saved her from the worst and when her results spoke for themselves. What ingratitude!

I knew there was a danger of my emotional state betraying me and making me lose my coach's self-assurance. I needed to take a step back and react calmly. I needed time, I needed not to offend her, I needed to stay as neutral as possible. It was a direct attack. Perhaps she was just provoking me. To respond to this provocation would be a mistake, especially as I could not control all the details.

An idea came into my mind: I had to let her reasoning take its course, to put her back against the wall. She was doubting my ways and was proposing others. However my methods were proven. What about hers? So I replied: "I think the type of game that I've asked you to play has produced results that are more than satisfying. But having said that, I'm open-minded and maybe you're right. It's possible that I haven't understood your game perfectly. This is what I propose: tomorrow I won't brief you before your match like I usually do. You are completely free to play whatever type of tennis you want. Show me your game style, I will try to understand it and we will talk afterwards." My reply seemed to bring back her smile. She would enjoy showing me what she knew she could do... or otherwise.

The match against Peng started. Within 45 minutes Nastia was trailing 1-6 2-5. Within a few moments the Chinese girl would be inflicting on my player her worst defeat for a year. She called me on to the court at the change of ends.

"I know what you're going to say to me!"

"That would surprise me because I don't know myself what I'm going to say."

"How many winners have you hit since the start of the match?"

"I don't know."

"I'll tell you: it's three. Now tell me how many winners she has hit."

"I don't know."

"Thirty–six. I've counted them. But that's no surprise. You're letting her dictate the game, you're hitting the ball without any intensity, you're playing the ball short. If she had played like that you would have hit 36 winners. There are two ways you can go: either you continue to play the way you've been playing since the start of the match, or you start to hit the ball."

With those words I returned to my seat. Nastia had been shaken by my intervention, but from that moment she reverted to being the player that I knew. She pulled the score back to 3-5, then 4-5, then 5-5. She took her Chinese opponent to a tie-break but ended up losing 7-6 after falling back into her shortcomings from the start of the match.

After the match she was dejected. I joined her. She asked me: "What did you think of the match?" I replied: "There's nothing to say, Nastia. What happened told its own story and I hope you will have drawn a lesson from it."

The young Russian did not want to carry on working, did not want to push herself through the pain barrier any more. Of course she would like to keep climbing up the rankings, but she was discouraged by the thought of the amount of work she would have to put in. There is a huge difference between "I would like" and "I want". In her case, Nastia had reached her comfort zone. She was making a very good living, was playing in all the world's biggest tournaments, was sponsored by some big brands, was in demand for photo–shoots, was being asked for her autograph and was highly regarded. If she was to go any higher, she had to want it badly, deeply. That desire has to come from right inside you and that clearly was not the case with Nastia. She was satisfied and was no longer putting in the work in training.

I told her that I was aiming much higher than the top 30. I said it was the second time that I had called her to order. I did not have any time to lose. I wanted to take her to the top and there was a price to pay for that. "I won't be talking to you like this for a third time. You won't be able to say that I didn't warn you."

The attitude I was taking was not that of a coach. I should have been looking for solutions to help her rediscover her motivation. I should equally have been showing patience. Perhaps she just needed three or six months for her motivation to return...

Perhaps she needed to be more mature, to learn from the experience of failure and to fall back down the rankings in order to understand what she really wanted, what her real ambitions were and the price she would have to pay.

Except that the very fact that she was satisfied with her ranking as it was told me something: there was a strong chance that she had reached her comfort zone. Champions are never satisfied. Finishing second is unacceptable to them. That, it seemed, was not the case with Nastia. It was therefore likely that she was not mature enough to be ready to win a Grand Slam title, at least not within the next two years. The strong probability was that my player would not enable me to realise my own ultimate goal.

That was a situation that I could not accept. As far as I was concerned, I had higher ambitions. I therefore preferred to be up-front with her and let her know that her lack of motivation was a handicap for me.

If she was not inclined to do what was necessary, I would respect her choice – but she would no longer be of interest to me.

After the US Open, having seen no sign of improvement, I took the decision to stop working with her.

9

Aravane – or extreme coaching

"Kill your enemies with your victories,
bury them with your smile."

Ziad K. Abdelnour

After the professional break–up with Nastia, I took a few months off for reflection. Several players, male and female, wanted me to work with them, but I could not see any of them offering me the possibility of reaching new milestones in my career. I preferred therefore to bide my time.

On several occasions over the last year I had coached Aravane Rezai at some important tournaments. Both the player and her family had confidence in me, to the point where they decided to base her at my academy. She had got used to working with one of my physical trainers and one of my physiotherapists.

I admired her a lot as a tennis player. She was an exceptional ball-striker, which was a result of the work she had done over many years with her father. However, I believed that she could still make much more progress and that she was falling way short of her potential. That made her all the more interesting.

She was a girl with a very engaging personality. She was almost permanently in a good mood and always looked on the bright side of things, as long as tennis was not involved. She was very interested in everything and everybody around her. She spent all her time with her brother, Anouch, who was her sparring partner, confidant and friend. They were very close and I was touched by their relationship. They were both very respectful and very well brought up. I liked working with Anouch. He listened intently, always tried his best and wanted to progress and to learn.

In October, when she was at Thiverval–Grignon preparing for the "Tournament of Champions" in Bali, a competition which brought together the players who had won one Grand Prix over the course of the year, she asked to see me: "Patrick, would you agree to come with me to this tournament? It's the most important tournament of the year for me and I'm the lowest-ranked player who will be taking part. It would help me a lot if you could coach me during this competition."

"I would like your father to be the one asking me."

"Okay, I will tell him."

I insisted on this point because I knew that for

this to work her father, the fearsome Arsalan, who terrorised the whole small world of tennis, would have to feel that he had taken the decision to request my presence. Besides, in putting him in a position where he was asking me, I would be opening up the scope of my work.

He quickly asked and I accepted. I was interested to see how she would get on and I was pleased at the thought of working with a French player. I love my country and like to play my part in improving the results of our athletes.

So there I was in Bali. I needed immediately to get Aravane into the best frame of mind to get the required result: to win. I knew her well enough to be able to use certain bits of information about her. She lived and travelled in a closed world with her brother and her parents. When we all sat down together for a meal, I suggested to Aravane that she and I should talk alone.

My attitude towards her and my words were hard. I set the tone straight away: "Aravane, I'm telling you now that I've not come to Bali for a holiday. If that was the case, I would not have come here with you."

"Of course. I know that."

"I've come here so that you can win the tournament."

We carried on talking to the point where she asked me if I would be disposed to continuing the coaching arrangement with her.

"Would you agree to becoming my coach?"

"I'll be very frank with you. I might be mistaken, but I sense that your level of motivation is not high enough in relation to my own standards."

I was provoking her. I wanted to know what she really felt inside. Her reaction was immediate. She broke down in tears.

"Yes, I am motivated. What are you thinking?"

"I've spent some time with you and from what I've seen you don't have enough motivation."

"Do you think I can get there?"

"Where?"

"To the top 10."

"What I do know is that if you carry on doing what you're doing for a few years, you have no chance. At the same time, it would be really worthwhile if you gave yourself the chance to make it. Then you would know. But for the moment, what you are putting in is way short of what is required."

"Okay. I'm not going to say anything. I will show you whether I am motivated or not. That would be better."

"That's absolutely fine by me."

The way had been paved. With that provocation, Aravane was in the right state of mind to go into this tournament. We would be able to work hard in order to be well prepared and she would be ready for the fight when she came to play her matches. She had so much to prove to me that I knew she would not give up on a single point and that opponents would have to kill her to beat her. My relationship with her parents was fluid and friendly. I like her family, who were very welcoming towards me. I discovered another, unsuspected side of Monsieur Rezai: he was droll, enthusiastic and likeable. As we understood each other well and he knew that I respected the work he had done over so many years with his daughter, he trusted me and gave me plenty of scope in which to work.

Having prepared extremely well for the tournament, Aravane hauled herself into the final, in which she would face Marion Bartoli, the French No. 1 and a member of the top 10. She was quickly down 4-1 against an opponent who exploited brilliantly the weakness of my player's second serves. When Aravane asked me to come for on-court coaching she was annoyed and upset: "I can't do anything. She's killing me on all my second serves!"

I sensed that she was looking for advice, but my modus operandi had been working well since the start of the tournament: I said it was up to her. I feared that if I gave her technical or tactical advice she would focus only on that and forget what was most important: to win.

I therefore replied: "If she's killing you on your second serves then you just need to serve better. You're not hitting the ball hard enough. You are too soft". I could see from the look on her face that I had hit the nail on the head. I had touched her pride and at the same time, without saying as much to her, had made her understand that she could do a lot better if she made the effort. And why not win?

The match changed completely and Aravane ended up winning. The trophy was hers, the ranking points would take her into the top 50 and the prize money would give her some breathing space. It had been a superb operation. But what she had gained above anything else – and this was what mattered most to her – was the possibility of working with me.

Aravane had been very impressive, yet I had never doubted her ability to climb mountains. She had both the game and the personality to do it. All that was required was for her to think in a way that would make her more efficient. Saying it like that might make it sound simple, but it requires very precise adjustments – like those of a Formula One car. And to put them into operation you have to know everything about the engine…

Her father made his official request to me the very next day. He saw that I had the influence over his daughter that was necessary in order to steer her towards a work regime that was more intense, more sustained and of better quality.

I accepted this arrangement on a full-time basis. I was ready for that. I immersed myself completely in the family's culture and decided to stay with them during tournaments. We ate together and even stayed in the same accommodation at places like Wimbledon, where they rented an apartment for the duration of the tournament. I also spent some time on my own with Aravane, including the whole of the American swing as her parents could not get a visa (because of their Iranian passports). I soaked up the maximum amount of information that I could, I ate their country's food and I learned and used some Iranian words.

I also agreed to give a helping hand to Yanina Wickmayer, but only when I had some free time, as I knew that Aravane was my priority. This Belgian player was one of my favourites. We achieved some excellent results together, even if I worked with her only intermittently and never on a one-to-one basis.

In March 2009 she reached No. 11 in the world rankings. I would have loved to work with her full-time for a long enough period to help her realise her potential. Her athletic qualities, her discipline and her huge capacity for work made her a unique individual. In addition we had established a relationship of real trust which always enabled us to reconnect very quickly and to work effectively as soon as we got back together.

Aravane was playing tournaments again and achieving respectable results. However, "acceptable" did not match my expectations. Despite everything, I knew that I owed it to myself to be patient while I found the best way of working with her.

All the same, she reached the semi–finals in Sydney, where she lost to Serena Williams, the world No 1, after leading 6–3, 5–2. She left the court with a smile on her lips. I asked her: "Why are you smiling?"

"Because I didn't think I would go so close to beating her."

"Well, you have just realised why you lost."

Aravane was surprised by Angelique Kerber in the second round of the Australian Open, then reached the last 16 at Indian Wells, fell in the second round at Miami and at the same stage in Rome to Yanina Wickmayer, whom I was also working with at the time.

However, that loss did not concern me as I had just finished putting together the last pieces of the puzzle. The overall picture was taking shape in front of my eyes. The upcoming event in Madrid was a big one, part of a group of tournaments that form the most important category after Grand Slams and which bring together the world's best players.

"Don't count the days. Make each day count."
Muhammad Ali

We travelled to Spain that day. On the day after we arrived I arranged to meet Aravane to discuss my plan of action. I had written it down but it was already very clear in my mind.

"Aravane, we've been working together for seven months now. It's time to draw up a balance sheet. Your results are decent enough, but you're not making the progress that I was expecting and that you're capable of."

"Because of the commitment I have to you I've let pass a number of interesting opportunities to work with top 20 players, even top 10 players, who wanted me to coach them. I don't have any regrets about that, because I think you can be better than them – but not if we carry on like this. There are therefore some changes we need to make."

"When we were in Bali you assured me that you were ready to make every effort necessary, even if you didn't understand what it was you were committing to. You have been making efforts. I'm aware of that. But we're still well short of what is required."

"So this is what I'm proposing to you today: I'm going to put in place for you a precise programme of work and strict rules which you must respect. If you accept that, we can carry on – and I can tell you that you will be very surprised by your world ranking at the end of the year. If you refuse, then I will not work with you any more."

I continued: "Here are the rules and how this is going to work out:

I will take absolutely all the decisions and I don't want to hear any comment from you or our collaboration will stop immediately.

I will tell you what time you will go to bed each evening, what time you will get up and what you will eat at every meal.

You will follow a strict diet. I want you to lose eight kilos. I will weigh you every Monday. You will need to have lost at least 500 grammes in comparison with the previous Monday. If you haven't lost that weight it will show that you have been cheating and eating forbidden foods on the quiet. If that happens, our relationship will end right away.

Your practice sessions will be much tougher. I will tell you exactly what I will be expecting of you. We will practise during tournaments as well. You will be competing for thirty weeks of the year. We can't contemplate losing thirty weeks of the year in which you could be making progress. I know that the majority of players spend most of their time at tournaments saving their physical energy for the day of their matches. What they are actually doing is "untraining" for thirty weeks of the year. We will do the opposite. Your physical training will also be more intense. At tournaments I will impose that you have some physical sessions on the days of your matches

When I brief you before your matches I will be very explicit about your game plan. I will tell you where to serve, where to return, at what height to hit the ball during rallies, and where to place the ball. I will also tell you where you should be positioning yourself on the court. I want you to follow these plans with absolute rigour. There will be no creativity from your side. You will be a robot who just carries out orders. You won't lose any matches playing like this, because I know all the players and I know how to beat them. You have the means at your disposal to do just that.

Before every match we will undertake a "rehearsal" during which you will go through all the patterns of play that you will need to use on a match day according to who your opponent is.

Your mobile phone will be in my pocket. You will use it only when I allow you to during the day and I will control your calls.

You will come with me to watch your opponents' matches in order to understand their game style, their strengths, their weaknesses and their favourite patterns of play.

If you fail to follow a single one of these rules our partnership will end immediately. I know that if you do it once and I let you get away with it, it will happen again. So there will be a zero tolerance policy.

For several long seconds Aravane did not respond. Tears ran down her cheeks. The facts hit her hard. At that moment she hated me and loved me at the same time. She was already visualising the suffering that I was preparing to inflict on her. The restrictions on her freedom, the intensity and the volume of the work that she was going to have to take on. But she also knew in her heart that I was offering her the chance to do what she had always dreamed of: to be successful at the highest level. She was too intelligent and too sensitive not to feel all of that – and I knew it. I was not surprised to see her crying. I had been expecting it.

She responded in an accusatory tone: "I don't have any choice other than to accept. It's the opportunity of a lifetime for me."

"Ask any questions you want. Now is the time to do that."

"Am I not going to be exhausted on court if you make me do physical training on the day of matches?"

"Yes, you will be tired, especially at the beginning. But it's something that you will need to get used to. You must learn to play when you're tired. When you're playing in the semi-finals of a Grand Slam tournament, you will be tired but you will have to win. This is a great experience for you and there will be no excuses. No other questions?"

"No. I accept. I told you, it's the chance of a lifetime for me. I won't let it slip."

From the next day I put my plan into operation.

Up at 7am and depart for the tournament venue for two hours of tennis practice on an empty stomach. Then a light snack: a glass of milk. After that, 45 minutes of jogging. In the afternoons, a session of intense physical preparation with a different theme every day: cardio, speed, core training or strengthening back and shoulders. And then a second two-hour tennis practice session.

The draw for the tournament was out. Aravane would be facing Justine Henin in the first round. Perfect! We would be in at the deep end from the start.

On the morning of the match, as I had warned, I got out one of my weapons of torture: a session of speed work using rubber speed bands. She suffered but did not utter a word. She had already got into a rhythm with the previous four days of training I had put her through.

Aravane lost the first set 6-4. Overall I was happy because she had followed the game plan. She had lost the set through a few small details, some oversights, some losses of concentration. But she stayed in touch in the second set. I gave her a lot of encouragement. I kept reminding her what she had to do: follow the game plan, keep following it, don't do anything else. Aravane discovered with astonishment that the strategy I had set out for her was working.

I had given her the weapons with which to beat the player who at that moment was the world No 1. Aravane could not get over it. I keep gazing at her during the match: "Stay focused. Don't get carried away. I know that you realise you can beat her, but you must stay calm and follow your tactics to the letter."

She eventually won the second set. Henin had been wounded. Some unknown minor opponent was outplaying her. At the end of the second set my player called me on to the court. I took the chance to give her some encouragement: "Keep following the plan. I don't want any creativity or personal input from you. We're not here to enjoy ourselves. We're here to win. Step further into the court. Move forward to hit the ball. Follow the plan – only the plan, nothing but the plan. And keep both feet into the court – like we do during practice."

The third set was a formality and signalled the end of Henin's domination. Aravane won it 6–0. From now onwards she had faith in my tactical plan and in her own abilities. She knew that she was being perfectly prepared and had a winning strategy. From this moment anything was possible.

She was exultant: "Unbelievable! I felt that I was playing only at 40 per cent and yet I beat Justine Henin!" I replied: "You simply played the right way and stayed close to your line. When you play like that you are very strong – stronger than her and the other players."

Her tournament was under way. What followed confirmed the corner she had turned: victories, only victories, all the way to the final, where she brushed aside Venus Williams, having beaten Andrea Petkovic and Jelena Jankovic along the way.

For the first time in her career, Aravane was in touching distance of her dream. She could not hold back her tears after converting match point in the final. She posed for photographs with Nadal, who won the men's title, and became an instant celebrity.

The sporting press were at fever pitch: a Frenchwoman who had won such an important title would surely have a chance at Roland–Garros! On her return to Paris she held a press conference. All the journalists wanted to watch her practice sessions. We had to keep cool heads. I took control of everything. I was keen to ensure that Aravane did not feel she had reached the top. It was vital that she maintained her desire.

"Being demanding is the ultimate form of kindness."

In the third round at Roland–Garros Aravane

unfortunately lost 8-6 in the third set to Petrova after a match which was spread over two days. It was a shame, because she'd had her chance to win the match. However, she was short on mental and physical freshness. Madrid had left its mark and she had not really had enough time to rest.

I will remember the scene when she left centre court after this merciless fight against her Russian opponent for the rest of my life. Aravane was dejected. I waited for her in the tunnel between Court Philippe–Chatrier and the locker rooms. When she arrived, she looked me in the eye, watching for my reaction. She was frightened about what it might be. She had lost, she was empty, because she had given everything. She was exhausted.

Her Roland–Garros adventure was over, as was this unbelievable run of victories she had been on. She felt weak: for all these reasons this was a distressing moment for her. I looked at her and told her: "I'm proud of you." In a flash her eyes filled with big tears which fell to the ground. She was happy. She knew that, more than anything, I respected what she had just done. I knew the effort that she had put in. She had already lost four kilos (she would lose eight in total), she had observed all the rules that we had put in place, she had worked harder than ever, she had put her heart and soul into every match, she had hit every ball in every practice session with the required focus. I had to teach her to do that, but she had learned.

She used to hit thousands of balls every day, but without thinking, without a specific goal, without the necessary focus. I did not allow any slacking at our practice sessions. Every time she struck a ball it had to be of a length and at a height over the net that I demanded. When she was hitting with her brother, Aravane had to play the correct shot every time, according to both where she was striking it and the speed of the ball. If that did not happen I would stop the exchange and I would be hard on her: "What are you doing exactly? Where should you have been hitting that ball?

"Cross–court?"

"Yes. So tell me why you didn't do that."

" …"

"You're not focused! I'm not going to tell you again!"

But that day at Roland–Garros, in the tunnel, when her tears were falling in large drops, I looked at her and I was so proud of her! I was proud of all the effort and all the sacrifices she had made. I was proud of the player that she had become. She had grown, she had changed in stature. Despite the defeat, in my eyes she was the stronger and better player that day.

Aravane went on to beat Caroline Wozniacki, the world No 1, at Eastbourne, lost in the second round at Wimbledon but won the title at Bastad the following week.

Aravane was No. 15 in the world and the French No. 2 after a vertiginous rise. She had lost a lot of weight to get down to 62 kilos, which was the right weight for her body. She moved like she never had before, stayed close to her line and made many fewer errors than she used to. Her tennis was rationalised and in good shape. However, it was important to remain focused and above all to carry on working hard. The road to the top of the rankings is a long one. It is a marathon, not a sprint.

Unfortunately Aravane had arrived at the end of her journey. Players' limits are neither tennis–related nor physical. For the most part they are mental. Their ambition drops and in the end they decide that the level they are at is not so bad after all.

Like Marcos or Nastia before her, Aravane was quite happy with her status. She was now earning good money. People knew who she was. They recognised her. Okay, she could continue to work hard, but what for? Am I ready to pay the price? Does what she has to gain, on top of what I have already, merit the amount of effort that would be required? To all these questions she gave the same reply: "I'm going to stay where I am in the rankings. I'm fine with that. But I no longer want to put in so much effort." She did not know it – because she did not want to know it – but that was what her sub–conscious was whispering into her ear.

"I'm tired. What you're making me do is inhuman."

"I recognise that it's difficult, but that is the price to be paid for being the best. Very few players are ready to make these sacrifices. That's one of the reasons why there is only ONE number one."

"I can no longer do what you're asking of me. Nobody could. That's the reason why your players don't stay with you for long."

"You're right. Ninety per cent of players are not capable of doing it. And that's the reason why they will never be number one. They pretend that they are ready for everything in pursuit of their so-called goal. I look at what they do on a daily basis and I tell you: they do not want to be number one, they would simply wish to be number one. There is a big difference."

"And what about me?"

"Until now you have done the job. I have no complaints. And I don't think you can't have any complaints either about it. The results have come. Now you have just told me that you will never be world number one because it's too hard. That's your right. I respect that. But I want to go right to the top. If you're not interested in doing that, I will have to find someone else. I've respected my deal with you 100 per cent. Your results have been beyond your expectations. You're letting me go in the middle of our journey yet you had said to me that you would stay with it to the very end. I'm disappointed, but that's life. I can't force you."

That conversation marked the end of our collaboration. Within a year Aravane had fallen to No. 120 in the world. A year later she was down to No. 250.

I was disappointed for her. She had impressed me during our time together. I had always believed in her, but she had shown me some exceptional qualities in terms of her game. Her ball-striking is unique. She has some real physical qualities. And above all, she has a big heart. If you know how to communicate with her, how to make a connection with her, she is capable of giving everything she has inside her.

I am very proud of what we achieved in our time together and she should be too. It was just a shame that our adventure came to an end.

Aravane did not show any emotion at that precise moment when our collaboration ended. She had certainly become more confident. I knew she was convinced that she would continue to progress by following the route that she had chosen. This was the future she had mapped out for herself: less training, less rigour, less sticking to a diet. She was sure about what she was doing and disappointed that I would not be following her down this path. She was angry with me. I understood everything that she was feeling. I knew her by heart. I also knew that we had a bond that was stronger than tennis. Throughout our time working together she always said: "Patrick is my second father."

I love Aravane deeply. She knows that she can count on me and that she holds a particular place in my life.

I had learned a huge amount from this adventure. I had become much more precise in my approach. I had developed a four–stage method of coaching which absolutely had to be followed in chronological order:

1. I am in charge of my own destiny.
2. I embrace what I teach.
3. I understand and enter my player's world.
4. I transform myself. I become the person they have been looking for all their life.

Having spent three years working with women, I then went back to the men's circuit. I like the variety. I like having to adapt. I don't want to be categorised as a coach of female players. Players see me at work every day and like my involvement, my motivation, my rigour. They also see that my players make a lot of progress. Several interesting players wanted me to work with them.

Jérémy Chardy called me during the Australian Open. Things weren't working out any more with his coach and his career was stalling. I agreed to help him for a few months so that he could pick himself up. He saved France's Davis Cup team from relegation a few months later by beating

Jürgen Melzer, who was in the world's top 10 at the time, in his first match and then winning the deciding rubber on the Sunday to clinch the tie.

I maintain a very strong connection with "Jim" and consider him to be one of my closest friends.

His generosity, his humour and his warmth are all qualities that I appreciate, just as I appreciate his idea of friendship. We have a very strong and very special connection. I have difficulty working with Jérémy because I find it difficult to go into "professional" mode with him as he is part of my personal world. I know I can always count on him if I need him. He knows equally that I will always be there for him.

After this spell of working with Jérémy I wanted to aim even higher in my coaching career. I felt that I needed to make a bigger impact; I needed to work with someone who could give me this chance. In February 2012 Grigor Dimitrov, a promising young player in world tennis, called me. I had known him for several years. I had picked him out at the Petits As tournament when he was thirteen. At that time I was coaching Marcos and I had invited Grigor to come to the academy for two weeks to practise with him. At the age of seventeen Grigor had rejoined us at Thiverval-Grignon.

When he parted company with Peter McNamara he turned to me.

I was convinced that this player, who had been nicknamed the Bulgarian Federer, was capable of winning Grand Slam titles. He has the technical assets, the natural qualities, the physical capacity, the ego and the necessary motivation. I like the human being that he is. He was straightforward to deal with, uncompromising, frank and generous, yet he was also a refined and complex character.

Our collaboration went very well. Grigor put total trust in me. As a sign of friendship, when he bought something he would often get two of them in order to give me the second of them by way of a present. I was happy with his results and he was making progress.

Grigor is a player who needs to feel totally in sync with his coach. I'm like him. We had an intense relationship. I understood his motivation, his doubts, his complexity. Unlike many people, I did not pass judgement on the young Bulgarian as I had learned to refuse to judge people on the basis of their behaviour. I believe that if any issues arise from someone's behaviour they can be dealt with as necessary. I thought that he had scope to improve in certain aspects in this area, which would enable him to make quicker progress. He liked my frankness and the way I interacted with him. He often told me that he appreciated my being straight with him, even if I refused to judge him. He could sense that I was keeping a benevolent eye on him but was being demanding at the same time.

The many occasions that we spent time together during tournaments were always special. I took a particular interest in noticing everything that brought emotions out of him: painting, house decoration. He got me to share his love of watches – and I am someone who is not in the slightest materialistic. I took an interest and could see what it was that appealed to him. It's something I've remained interested in ever since. I also discovered the states of mind that he went through and in which he found comfort: melancholy or, in contrast, euphoria. He regularly alternated between the one and the other.

In March, during the Miami tournament, we were together at a restaurant. A big celebrity came in, accompanied by a friend: Serena Williams. She knew Grigor well and came over to our table. She chatted with us for five minutes before going over to her own table for dinner.

I was immediately struck by her aura, her charisma, and by the huge difference between what she represents and on the other side, her very unaffected manner and her sense of humour.

Roland-Garros 2012. On the day before the tournament all the players were ready to begin the fight. At the venue the tension was palpable. From now onwards the athletes would be very focused. I left Grigor in the locker room and waited outside for him.

Serena came out of the women's locker room. She saw me and came over to talk: "How are you? Everything okay? Who is Grigor playing in the first round?"

"Donald Young. How about you?"

"I'm playing a French girl: Razzano. I often play French opponents here at Roland-Garros."

"You usually don't do too badly against them… I hope you have a good match."

To contextualise the situation, Serena had ruptured ankle ligaments in 2010. She had one surgery but then needed another because the first had not gone as well as had been hoped. Early in 2011 she was rushed to hospital, having suffered a pulmonary embolism. She could have been dead within a day. After a subsequent break she had started playing tournaments again, but had not won another Grand Slam title. So here she was at Roland-Garros…

Serena ended up loosing to Virginie Razzano – a shocking result to say the least. I remember the moment very clearly: I was in the Eurosport studios when the match was taking place. A group of people were standing around the screen as the first great surprise of the tournament unfolded.

My feelings were split between a deep affection that I felt for Virginie and the immense respect that I had for the American champion. I could not recognise Serena. In terms of her game it was obvious that she did not produce the tennis she was capable of, while on a mental level she was unrecognisable. She was negative and seemed lost out on court; she was in tears at every change over and gave the impression that she had already lost and that obviously was the outcome.

Grigor, for his part, won his first round and put up a huge fight against Richard Gasquet before losing in four sets in his second round match. He gave everything he had. After one unbelievable rally Richard vomited on court while Grigor collapsed, paralysed by cramp and could only crawl back to his chair. It was a dramatic scene that you rarely witness on a tennis court. It has gone around the world on *YouTube*.

The following week I stayed in Paris, as I had agreed with Grigor, who went with his father to play a Challenger tournament on grass. I needed to spend a week at home to see my children as I had been away so much since the start of the year. I had work to do at the academy. In particular I had to watch the tennis students play matches and receive the reports from their teachers. The telephone rang: "Hello, it's Serena. How are you?"

"I'm okay. How about you? I hope that defeat wasn't too hard for you."

"It was. It was very hard to take. I'm staying in Paris. I need to practise. Can you find somewhere for me?"

"I know the best place in the world to practise. It's called the Mouratoglou Tennis Academy."

"Ha ha! Why not? It's not far, is it?"

"No."

"Could I have two sparring partners on court

with me?"

"Okay. I'll send a car to your place at 11 tomorrow to bring you to the academy. I'll be waiting for you with two sparring partners. See you tomorrow."

"See you tomorrow."

My coaching method was elaborated on by working alongside
the best junior and professional players over the last twenty years.
Here, I am hitting with Grigor Dimitrov in 2012.

Marbella (Spain), 1989.
Winner of the tournament.

Montreuil 1998.
The beginning of the
Bob-Brett Academy.
Here with Bob himself.

With Irena Pavlovic in 2004,
who had just won the under 16 French National Championships.

US Open 2005. Training session with Marcos Baghdatis and André Agassi.

With Marcos Baghdatis who won the Orange Bowl
back in 2003 and became Junior World Champion.

At the Australian Open in 2010 with Yanina Wickmayer.

With Yung-Jan Chan and her doubles partner
who won the Rome tournament back in 2008.

Alongside Aravane and Anouch Rezaï in 2010.
Aravane had just won the Madrid Open.

With Anastasia Pavlyuchenkova at Indian Wells in 2009.

With Jérémy Chardy
at Roland Garros in
2011.

With Martina Hingis.
Pre-season 2011,
Mauritius.

Explaining the
training exercises to
Grigor Dimitrov
during pre-season in
Mauritius in 2011.

With Richard Williams in Miami in 2006 during an interview with him I conducted for the magazine *L'Equipe*.

With Serena Williams after she won her 19th Grand Slam title in Australia in 2015.

With Serena Williams celebrating her two gold medals at the London Olympics back in 2012.

My goal: to help my players push their limits to make their dreams come true.

10
Serena, our adventure

*"You don't reach your goal by walking
only on the days when the sun shines."*

Chinese proverb

I had the feeling that my whole life had prepared me for this meeting.

Firstly, I had chosen this job with an eye on one day working with the best in order to enter the realms of the highest competition. In football every coach dreams of seeing their name associated with Real Madrid, Manchester United or Bayern Munich. Because with these teams you can set out in search of the biggest, most magnificent, ultimate reward – the Champions League. I knew that the day would come when I had proved myself sufficiently for a male or female champion to call on me.

Besides, I had always had immense respect for this player. To me, Serena represents the ultimate champion. Her capacity for work, her formidable self-confidence, her ability to intimidate her opponents with her charisma and her refusal to be beaten make her a totally unique player. She embodies the values of the very highest level better than anyone else in the world of women's tennis. When I've spoken to young players I have always cited her as the example to follow.

In 2006 *L'Equipe* magazine commissioned me to interview Richard Williams, the father of Serena and Venus. We talked for two hours, during which time he told me how he had turned his two girls into champions. During the photo shoot, the photographer asked him to throw a ball towards me in a gesture which was supposed to symbolise a passing of the baton. A premonition?

In 2012, the day after her phone call, Serena arrived at the academy's reception. I greeted her and we headed off to the court. Having warmed up, she started to hit some balls. She carried on doing so for thirty minutes without pausing once. The movement of her head and her expressions showed her discontent. She was trying to find her tennis. I didn't move and didn't speak. I placed myself where the umpire's chair would have been, without a racket, just observing. She eventually came over to her chair to take a break and have a drink. Two minutes later she turned to me and shouted out in English: "Talk to me!" I walked over to her. I had five seconds to think. What I was about to say would perhaps be the most important words of my professional career. I had to get it right.

"I watched your match against Razzano. I can see that you're making the same mistakes in practice that I saw you make in your match. You're not respecting the fundamentals. You're waiting for the ball to come to you instead of moving towards it. And when you hit the ball you're not balanced. Your feet need to be further apart and your centre of gravity needs to be lower at the moment of contact with the ball to give you better stability."

"That's unbelievable! My father also tells me that I don't move up to the ball."

For the first time that morning, a smile broke out on her face.

"Can we work on that?"

"Yes, let's go."

I stood in front of her and started to throw balls at her: "We'll start by doing things right, slowly. When we're satisfied with the result, we'll accelerate the tempo."

After a two-hour session she stopped. She was visibly satisfied with the outcome.

"Can we carry on with this work over the next few days?"

"Yes, with pleasure. I'll send someone to pick you up at 11 o'clock tomorrow."

The next day we had another productive and interesting practice session. Serena's game was improving and I felt that she was liking the way we were working.

"I'm supposed to leave tomorrow but I'd like to carry on for a few more days. When are you available until?"

"I'm leaving next Monday to join up with Grigor at Queen's."

"Great, I will delay my flight."

I shifted up a gear the next day. I wanted to gather all the information I could to help with our work. I told Serena that I wanted to move forward with her in a more professional manner. I explained that I worked with a physiotherapist and a physical trainer. The physiotherapist produces reports which build a precise picture of each player's body: the strong points, the weak points, areas which need strengthening, areas which need stretching. The idea is to act early by taking preventative action to stop injuries happening. The physical trainer then carries out a number of additional tests to measure strength, speed and cardio. I also make a full report to him of what I observe on the tennis court. As a result he has at his disposal all the information he needs to draw up a plan for both injury prevention and physical development. I also have a doctor specialising in nutrition and physiology who does regular blood checks on my players to make sure they are not suffering from any deficiencies.

Serena was open to all of that and was happy to go along with it.

We started all the tests the following day. The

results showed an important iron deficiency, which would have been one of the likely causes of her general tiredness. The other tests revealed some malfunctions which explained the number of injuries she had been suffering. Without interrupting what we were doing on the court, we started on the preventative work the same day.

On the following Sunday I flew to London to rejoin Grigor at the Queen's Club tournament. When the tournament finished it was time to prepare for Wimbledon. Like many other players, we decided to practise on–site in order to get used to playing on the grass. It was then that I received a phone call from Serena: "Hi Patrick. I'm arriving at Wimbledon tomorrow afternoon. I'd like to meet and have a chat."

"We could meet the day after tomorrow if you want."

"No. I arrive tomorrow. I want to see you tomorrow! Can we meet in a café at the end of the afternoon to talk?"

"Okay."

On the day of the meeting, I waited for Serena in the agreed location. She arrived half an hour late. She was in a happy and playful mood and seemed very happy to see me again. But after the usual greetings her look changed. She was on a mission and very focused, though at the same time she maintained this seemingly relaxed appearance in order to keep me at ease.

"I'm ready to train hard. I've been feeling better on the court since we started working together. I'd like to talk to you about something. I'd like us to do Wimbledon together, as a start. I'd like to do the tournament as a trial with you."

She immediately continued: "I haven't won a Grand Slam tournament for a good while. I'm absolutely determined to get back to the top. I'm ready to do whatever's necessary to achieve that. I've only ever had one coach: my father. Perhaps the moment has come for me to have another look at my game. I like your way of working and I'm certain that with you I can get back to the top. We don't know each other well yet, but what I have seen makes me want to take this further. I like your energy. You give out a feeling of strength. When you're in the room, even if you are not doing or saying anything, you have a presence. You also exude a feeling of confidence that makes me want to have you by my side. I absolutely want to win Wimbledon. I have to erase the memory of what happened in the first round at Roland-Garros. I'm ready to make every sacrifice in order to win. Tell me how I can do that."

"Well firstly, thank you for your confidence in me. I'm proud and touched by it. The idea of working with you in order for you to become the great Serena again is obviously very motivating.

"But despite this, I have to remind you that I am working with Grigor. I have a commitment to him.

He is, moreover, someone I like a lot and someone in whom I have great belief. I need his agreement. I'll talk to him when we get back this evening.

"As for what you're proposing to me, this is how I see things: firstly, I think that if you prepare in the right way there is no reason why you should ever lose a match. You're capable of winning the vast majority of the tournaments you enter. We can make our preparations with this in mind."

"Second thing: you need a Plan B. When all the lights are green and you're playing your best tennis, nobody can beat you. When you go into the big matches, the big finals, you have this ability to raise your game above everyone else's. Except that you're not at the top of your form every day of the year. You have to have a Plan B in place for those other days. To achieve that we need to work on your tennis to increase the number of options you have in your game to enable you to win."

"I like the sound of that. At the same time I have to tell you that I'm a very bad loser. When I lose I go into a depression for several days afterwards. I don't even get out of my bed."

"You don't need to warn me about that. That situation is not going to arise."

Serena was taken aback. She thought about it and then replied: "You're right."

With those words we parted. I knew that what I said had resonated with her, even if, throughout our conversation, she had tried not to let anything show. It was this face, which she constantly wore which led me to give her the nickname "Pokerface". I broached the subject with Grigor that very evening: "Do you remember that I worked with Serena for a week in Paris?"

"Yes of course."

"Today she asked me if I could work with her at Wimbledon this year. I told her that I was committed to you and that you are my priority. I'd like to know what you think about this."

"I think it's something that would be very interesting for you. You must do it. If you promise me that nothing will change as far as I am concerned, and that you will always be there when I need you, I'll agree to it."

"Without fail. If you're both practising at the same time, I'll be with you, not her. Same thing if you're playing matches at the same time. You will always be the priority."

From the next day onwards I was out on the court with Serena. I was pleased to see that she spared no effort. It was time to put the plan into operation, but what she didn't know was that for the moment it would be different to the plan I had told her about. What I had actually come up with was a short-term plan to start with, because for the moment my only aim was for her to win Wimbledon. From the moment when she had started hitting balls at the academy I had appreciated the extent to which she was lacking in confidence. If I could pull off this gamble, she would rediscover her confidence and her tennis. Then would be the time to put in place my long–term strategy.

> *"If you fail to plan, you plan to fail."*
> Benjamin Franklin

As had been the case with Nastia, in order to re-establish confidence you have to improve the way you manage stress emotionally. I therefore put together a plan for Serena to win Wimbledon in 2012 which could be broken down into four parts:

1. Re–establish her confidence.
2. Deal with her stress.
3. Make her more efficient in matches.
4. Rebuild a major weapon.

1. Re–establish her confidence
The defeat in the first round at Roland-Garros had sapped her confidence in her tennis, which had already been undermined by her failure to win any Grand Slam titles in the previous two years. Serena cannot accept defeat, which leaves her hugely frustrated. On the court that frustration comes out in the form of tension which is very damaging.

As I could sense the great faith that she had in me, I knew that my attitude and everything I said would have an effect – either positive or negative –

on her level of confidence.

When she asks me what she should be doing, what she actually wants is to know whether I believe in her. She wants to hear me say that she is still a champion. In the event, I had no doubt about that. I had huge confidence in her capabilities, in her ball–striking power and overall aptitudes. Behind the player who was going through a temporary moment of weakness I could still see the champion. My opinion put her in a different frame of mind. She could see that I did not have any doubts, which in turn gave her great strength. At this precise moment in her career that was what she needed. I always consider my players to be the best. I am convinced that they will become number one and I try to convey this energy to them. My certainty was even stronger as far as this great champion was concerned. For me Serena is still the best; to prove that to other people was a question only of time.

In order to achieve that she needed to be more consistent in her play. A loss of confidence distorts what a player feels during a match. Stress brings nerves and anxiety. Unwittingly, morale drops, the footwork becomes more hesitant, and the racket does not hit through the ball. The legs, made heavy by tension in the muscles, do not work as well or as quickly or as precisely. The weight of the body involuntarily falls backwards at the moment when the player strikes the ball. These automatic reflexes feed off each other and become an established part of your game. I had to put back in place the fundamentals of her game.

With this in mind we had to work on her stability when she hits the ball and her follow-through. I got her to move forward and asked her to make her racket stay in contact with the ball for longer. I knew that would give her more feel for the ball and thus better control. That in turn would help to reduce her anxiety as she would be striking the ball better. The cocktail started to take effect. The confidence that she gradually rediscovered in her game was reinforced by the presence by her side of a coach in whom she believed and who believed in her.

2. Deal with her stress
In order to get her back to winning ways I had to free her from the stress that was causing her to despair.

Establishing a mid-term perspective
Serena's need to win in order to feel reassured was not healthy. At this stage of her career it was even counter–productive. In order to lighten her load I decided to give her a mid-term perspective. That would reduce the anxiety she was feeling. In suggesting to her targets which were further down the line, I was authorising short-term losses. What I told her was simple: you will become the player

you were once again and you will even be stronger than ever. We will work at it. It will take a few months. We must be patient. This "right to lose" allowed her to relax, both mentally and physically. She gave herself the scope to take risks and express herself on court. Accepting, on a temporary basis, the idea of defeat freed her from her anguish.

Perfect preparation

I believe that the best way to combat harmful stress is to prepare well and to go into a match feeling that you have done your work.

Like a student sitting an exam, a player has no room for mistakes and is judged against other people. To go into an exam when you are not properly prepared is a very difficult experience; maybe you have not had enough time to learn everything or you have deliberately skipped over parts of your subject in the hope that you will not be asked about them. You go into the exam with fear in your stomach. Stress is at a peak. Whereas perfect mastery of the subject all but removes any feelings of anxiety.

That was the phenomenon that I wanted to produce for Serena. Thanks to the time she had spent on court, the quality of her focus and the appropriateness of the technical adjustments she had made, her game was returning with every passing day. She felt ready and capable of winning, solid in her game and in her preparations.

Provide more information

For most of us, we generally evolve in our own "comfort zone". When there is any change in our lives, no matter how minor, the fear of coming out of this zone creates significant emotional tension, because it suggests that you are entering unknown territory.

A professional tennis player's journey requires to leave that comfort zone on a regular basis. Competition effectively calls her into question every day. She travels across the world, has to deal with different environments and faces all types of players. She cannot be certain about the playing conditions, about her own form, about what her opponent will be like, or the quality of her own performance when D–day arrives. In this stressful environment, the player falls back on her routines and surrounds herself with people whose behaviour she is totally familiar with. She creates a reassuring environment for herself.

I always strive to extend my players' comfort zones. Because the unknown can produce anxiety, I provide them with as much information as possible in order to give them the feeling that they are going into familiar territory. Setting out alone into a completely alien world is not a pleasant experience. However, if someone reliable has told you beforehand what you are going to find and as a consequence you have a clear picture of the environment you are heading into, you feel less emotional tension.

That is one of the objectives of my pre-match briefings. Often times, the opponent is an unknown quantity. Even if my player has already faced her, I endeavour to help my player to read her game better and to know more about how she acts. For example, I will tell my player that her opponent systematically hits her second serves to the backhand; that she tries to hit down the line very early in a rally in order to avoid cross-court backhand exchanges, which make her feel uneasy; or that when she faces break points when serving into the advantage court she serves down the "T". All these pieces of information help my player to anticipate her opponent's game and not be surprised. She feels more at ease, because this is a familiar territory to her.

3. *Make her more efficient in matches*
The other objective of my pre-match briefing is to increase my player's efficiency in competition. I divide things into three sections: information, tactics and conditioning.

Information
As I have just explained, I am adamant that my player must go on the court with a precise picture of what his opponent will be like.

During the match, the more information that my player has on her opponent the better placed she is to anticipate the rival's shots and the more chance she has of winning. The ability to surprise an opponent is a formidable attacking weapon in this sport. By giving my player some keys with which to read her opponent's game, I am taking away that opponent's ability to surprise.

All my players go on the court knowing where their opponents generally place their serves in each service box, on both first and second serves, what their opponents' strengths and weaknesses are, their usual playing patterns and those patterns in which they are at their most uncomfortable, how they handle important points in terms of where they serve and their shot patterns, how they behave on court, their playing style and where they most like to hit the ball.

In the course of my ten years on the professional circuit I have carefully observed every female player in various matches against different opponents. I have a little notebook, which I guard preciously, in which I make my notes about every one of them.

At the end of every match I enter all this information into individual files, one for every opponent. I keep dozens of hours of recordings of each match played by every player on the circuit. I have also set up my own statistical charts which provide me with concrete statistical information which I use to devise winning strategies. I have great belief in statistics, because they are based on facts rather than emotion.

Anyone watching a tennis match does so with their appreciation of it coloured by a whole range of ideas: their own concept of this sport, their own perception of the player in question... Subjectivity is a filter through which data is distorted. I always verify my own impressions by matching them up against the statistical evidence.

In tennis today coaches' decisions are made all too often on the basis of subjective perceptions. There is no attempt to confirm the accuracy of any analysis or to be more precise about it.

I am convinced that the next revolution in the world of coaching will come through the use of statistics. Statistics are already used in the United States in sports where the financial stakes are high, namely baseball, basketball and American football. The use of multiple cameras, in combination with the use of relevant statistics, can give you an understanding about the trajectory of balls, about the contact point or about different areas of the court. Thanks to these tools I think our profession will change. The next generation of these tools will be capable of producing a complete and precise analysis of individual players and the way they play. The coach will then be able to concentrate on the essential part of his job: working on the mental game and drawing up strategies.

Tactical plan

Once I have broken down her opponent's game and explained it precisely to Serena, I move on to the tactical plan.

The general idea is to focus her efforts on the opponent's weak points: to give the opponent the sort of balls which will make her play short in the rallies and thereby create the optimal conditions in which Serena can attack. Tennis today is extremely sophisticated on the technical level. It is vital to have at your disposal weapons with which you can react to each game situation your opponent is able to create. At the same time, if your opponent has not been properly prepared from a technical point of view, she will not have the tools they need to stand her ground. The greater the range of shots at Serena's disposal, the more tactical options she will have available to her. That is one of the reasons why I am always endeavouring to provide her with additional weapons.

Before every match I tell her the zones where she should be hitting most of her serves, on both first and second serve, as well as what type of spins. Then, when the point is under way, she knows what is the best height and speed to hit the ball, whether she is hitting a forehand or a backhand.

One day Serena asked me something about an opponent she was preparing to play: "What is her strong point, backhand or forehand?"

"That question doesn't make sense."

"How come? It must do."

"Well let's just say that I can't give a simple answer."

"Okay then, explain."

"The money maker shot is her backhand. She hits more winners with the backhand, but she also makes more errors with it. She is very comfortable when her opponent hits the ball hard and flat, which is what most players do, which makes her dangerous with that particular shot. At the same time she is not comfortable when she is having to hit the ball at shoulder height. She tends to retreat a long way behind the baseline when she has to deal with these balls, which makes her vulnerable because she loses ground and hands her opponent control of the rally.

On her forehand the reverse is true. She hits the ball well at shoulder height; when dealing with slow, high balls she likes to run round her backhand to play this shot. At the same time, when the ball is coming fast and flat on to her forehand she tends to hit a lot of balls short, giving her opponent opportunities to attack. She is more efficient when she has to run to hit a backhand because she gets herself into position to play the ball better than she does on the forehand side, though she tends to hit down the line a lot when she gets tired. She's also a player who anticipates a lot, so it's good to wrong–foot her."

So in this actual case this was the game plan that

I proposed to Serena: "Hit most of your first serves to her forehand without much slice so that you can hit them at maximum speed. Be ready to attack her return, because she will often hit the ball short. Vary the direction of your second shot. Wrong-foot her frequently by hitting again to her forehand.

On your second serve, hit a kick serve high to her backhand and prepare to attack on the next ball. When you're in a neutral position in the rallies, attack her forehand to make her hit a short ball. When she's attacking and you're defending, play high to her backhand, which will push her back and enable you to regain possession of the court. From time to time surprise her by hitting hard to her forehand. When she is serving, attack her forehand with a lot of your returns and be prepared to move forward with your next shot.

When she tries to end a cross-court exchange on the forehand by going down the line, foil her by hitting hard to her forehand again. If she hits short when going down the line, step into the court, take the ball early and hit cross-court, wide to her backhand. If that doesn't win the point, cover your forehand side because she will try to counter down the line."

Mental conditioning
The quality of a player's performance in competition depends directly on his or her mental state. Of course it's imperative to go on court with

perfect knowledge of your opponent and with a precise game plan, but in order to express yourself best on a tennis court your must also be in the best possible frame of mind.

A player's psychology is linked to the general context of her (or his) professional life (she might be feeling positive or he could be in a period of self–doubts) and her personal life (she might be happy, in love, in a state of depression or at odds with those close to her).

That psychology is also influenced at the same time by short–term factors: how she is feeling in practice, what she thinks about her opponent (for example a player who gives her a problem, or equally a player she regularly beats), the general playing conditions (wind, heat, humidity, altitude, the make of the balls…).

And finally, her state of mind is also dependent on the pressure she is feeling. For example, if she is in the process of renegotiating her endorsement contracts she will need to prove her potential and will feel greater pressure than usual, which can be a positive or a negative depending on the player. On the other hand, if she is facing a big–name opponent and feels she has nothing to lose, she will probably play in a much more relaxed frame of mind.

The player is not aware of these internal conflicts which affect both her state of mind and, consequently, how well she will play in a match.

It is down to the coach to take these factors into account and to re-establish the player's psychological equilibrium.

When I brief Serena on the day of a match I tend to know exactly what her state of mind is. What I say is designed to put her into her "state of excellence" in the minutes before the start of the match. In order to do that I have to find the right words and convey the right messages. When you are coaching there are some truths which should not be expressed, because what always matters – and indeed this is the only thing that matters – is my player's perception of reality.

4. Rebuild a major weapon

The basics of her game were back in place, but Serena had not completely recovered her efficiency. The tension caused by some lingering anxiety was restricting her wrist just before she hit the ball. It was affecting her timing and the purity of her ball-striking. As a consequence she was less assertive and less powerful than normal.

I was aware that she absolutely had to have some decisive weapons at her disposal in order to win a Grand Slam title. I decided to concentrate on her serve, a shot which comes so naturally to her.

If she could totally recover her efficiency on this shot, she would be able to hold her serve, which would allow her to take risks on her opponent's serves and thus apply pressure.

From theory to practice

The strategy worked perfectly. During that Wimbledon of 2012 Serena broke all the serving records.

She hit more aces during the tournament than all the men in the main draw of the singles (even though they play best-of-five sets while the women play best-of-three) – a spectacular and unique record! The quality of her serve enabled her to keep her head above water in the early rounds and her tennis improved as the matches went on and she felt increasingly assured about her game. She went into matches in a satisfactory frame of mind and had fewer doubts. Serena Williams was back.

However, the early days at Wimbledon did bring a number of problems for me. My arrival at the heart of her team was not welcomed by everyone. It created a lot of jealousy, especially as Serena put great trust in me from the start. After her victory in the second round, when she beat Yaroslava Shvedova 7-5 in the third set, I was waiting for Serena in the fitness room to help her go through her recovery routine. Her father came into the room and was very wound up: "What's happening to her?" he asked me in an aggressive tone of voice. He was clearly unhappy with his daughter's performance. She was unwell that day. She had not told anybody except me. I did not like his tone of voice and replied: "I don't know."

Angered by my reply, he raised the tone of his

voice even further: "You must know! You're the coach! I'll ask again: what's happening to her?"

"Look, I don't like the way you're talking to me. I respect you. You must respect me too. If you want me to reply to your questions in the future you'll have to speak differently to me."

In the background I noticed Serena's sparring partner, who was making signs at me and seemed to be panicking.

Richard Williams continued: "For me tennis is business and everyone must be responsible for their own actions and do their own job."

"Believe me, you've got the right man. I accept all my responsibilities and I have no problem about being accountable. However, I don't share your view of tennis."

"Really? So what is tennis for you?"

"I'm not in this profession for the money. I have only sporting objectives. My only aim is for Serena to win Grand Slam titles."

He smiled and shook my hand. He had heard what he wanted to hear. He had tested me. He had put me under pressure so that he could better understand my personality. I recognised what he was doing. He had always coached his two daughters and probably needed to know what I was made of before handing over to me in the knowledge that his beloved daughter was in good hands.

When I had interviewed him he had explained to

me the whole strategy he had put together for his two daughters from their very earliest years. He had put in place a precise plan which he had always scrupulously followed.

To start with two children and to lead both of them to the top of the world rankings in a sport as competitive as women's tennis is a completely unprecedented achievement. This man will forever have a place in the history of our sport. I have immense respect for him and what he has achieved, but I had to establish my territory and stand my ground.

"Only those who will risk going too far
can possibly find out how far one can go."
— T S Eliot

After this episode I believed that I could at last work in serenity… but I did not know Serena. She in turn would go on to test me! The following morning she went on court. I said hello to her. She did not look at me, did not reply and went to sit down in order to put on her ankle braces. The practice session started. I told her what to do. She did not utter a word. The whole practice session went by in this atmosphere. She remained distant and aloof towards everyone who was there. At the end of the session, when she was sitting on her chair and tapping away on her phone, I hit her sharply on her cap. She gave a start and looked at me.

"I have some rules which have to be respected. Rule number one: when you arrive in the morning, you must say hello to me. Rule number two: when I talk to you, you must look at me and you must reply."

"Is that all?"

"For the moment, yes. If there are any more rules I will let you know."

I knew that I was taking a risk. She might have dug her heels in and sent me packing, ending our collaboration. But I needed to ensure that I was respected. As Bob Brett told me: "To be a good coach you must always be prepared to lose your job. If you live in fear, you won't dare to take the right decisions and you will be weak."

On that day I appreciated that I was a strong coach. I had been able to impose myself on a champion who possessed spectacular charisma. Serena still talks to me today about that episode, because I am one of very few people who have stood up to her.

Being ready to take risks is equally the mark of the great players. In the semi-finals of the US Open Serena double-faulted on an important point by going for an attacking second serve, Her sparring partner became animated. "Why did she do that?" he said. "She has lost some big matches by making mistakes like that. She should have just made sure that she put her second serve in court! That was a mad and pointless risk to take! Her opponent might have made an unforced error!"

"You're remembering the losses. I remember the number of matches that she has won by taking risks at the right moment, by taking her chance. She doesn't play with fear in her stomach. She plays to win."

A coach owes it to himself to follow the same path. To win the big battles, you must be ready to lose. That allows you to be daring, to be a person of action, to take your future into your own hands rather than simply living in expectation. Win or lose – but decide. If you don't, someone else will do it for you. That is my philosophy of life and it is one that Serena has always shared.

During that Wimbledon of 2012, she joined me in the players' restaurant after she had won her fourth–round match.

"Patrick! Whatever happens, I will be world number five at the end of the tournament."

"Yes. So what?"

"Aren't you happy about that?"

"No. Forgive me, but I couldn't care less."

"Pardon?"

"For someone like you, being number five in the world is just a stage to go through. It's not the final goal. I won't be happy until you're number one."

Serena was surprised by my reply. She was not expecting that sort of reaction from me. She did not know me yet.

That same evening she sent me a text message: "You're right about the rankings. I don't even understand how I could have been happy about it. Number five is worthless. Even number two is worthless. Number one or nothing!"

I would now discover whether my strategy would work in the long term. Serena had won both the singles and the doubles at Wimbledon. The tables were turning in our favour and she was becoming very dangerous. I had gambled on some victories to get her back on track and they had come off. Now I could put in place the development plan which I had proposed to her before the tournament.

Before anything else it was imperative that I had another discussion with Grigor to make sure that he wasn't unhappy about the situation. I met up with him when I returned to the academy; he assured me again that he had not changed his mind. I concentrated on him in the weeks that followed. He reached the semi-finals at both Gstaad and Bastad.

Between 28 July and 5 August 2012 Serena played at the Olympics and won the gold in both singles and doubles by playing exceptional tennis. Grigor lost in the second round to Gilles Simon.

Both players then went to play on the American swing without me. I had personal matters to attend to in August. My wife and I were separating after 17 years together. It was a huge upheaval, because we had shared everything over the years, during which time she had been unswervingly supportive of me. She had followed me everywhere on my travels with our two daughters for the best part of ten years and had always encouraged me in everything I had undertaken.

I rejoined Serena and Grigor at the 2012 US Open. My relationship with the American champion had grown stronger.

During this tournament I sensed that Grigor, mentally, was no longer on his game. One of the strengths of our partnership had been the connection between the two of us. Now the time that we spent together was not as good. Grigor is a very intuitive and sensitive guy and he did not cope well with the situation. Serena, maintaining her great momentum, won the tournament. In the space of two and a half months she had won the titles at Wimbledon, the Olympics and the US Open!

After the American swing I returned to France and took my children on holiday.

A few days after we had left, Grigor called me: "I'd like to talk. Where are you?"

"I'm on holiday with my children."

"Can I come and see you?"

"Yes, of course, but I'm 200 kilometres outside Paris."

"That's no problem. I'm coming."

I had already realised that he was not coping well with the present situation. He wanted to see me because he wanted to end our professional relationship.

We met the following day in a cafe. He was tense and did not try to hide the fact. I thought what he was doing was brave. I was sad at the idea of losing him, but I remained proud of his bravery and his ability to take responsibility. He would feel better when he had said his piece, so he went straight to the point: "I feel very uneasy in our situation. It has become worse and worse for me. I can't carry on like that. You know me by heart. You know that I need to be happy in order to play tennis. Well I'm not happy any more. But I can't bring myself to ask you to stop working with Serena. That would be too selfish of me given her results."

"You're a real man. You've come 200 kilometres to come and see me and tell me that to my face – but coming from you that doesn't surprise me. If you're finding the situation difficult, I completely understand your decision. At the same time, I've asked you frequently if you were okay with the situation."

"I know. I didn't judge things well. I didn't give myself the right to stop you doing what you did. I thought that I would move on, but I haven't been able to. I'm going to have to leave the academy. Believe me, that's a difficult thing for me to do. I'm very attached to the academy. For three years you have been like family for me. But I know that for the moment it would not be possible for me to be happy there."

We shared a long embrace. There is a lot of love between us, and immense mutual respect. I felt like crying. I know he did too. However, our pride stopped that happening.

The adventure with Serena continued. She was not going to play the Asian swing. She needed to resume practice. We started to put in place the second part of my strategy.

October brought the final tournament of the year. The WTA Championships, which used to be called the Masters, brought together the world's top eight players. Serena won again and finished the year ranked number three in the world.

The second part of the season had been exceptional in terms of results and 2013 got off to a similar start. Serena won the Brisbane tournament in January, but unfortunately she suffered an injury. A sprained ankle hampered her movement on the court and she lost in the quarter-finals of the Australian Open.

It was in Doha, in February 2013, after her semi-final victory over Kvitova, that she returned to the top of the world rankings. Emotion overcame her that day and she broke down in tears on the court. From March onwards she put together a record number of victories. She won in succession the tournaments in Miami, Charleston, Madrid, Rome and… Roland-Garros, where she won the title for the first time in ten years. Thirty-four wins in a row!

By some margin it was the longest winning run of her career; her previous longest had been twenty-three matches.

She went on to win Bastad and was unbeaten on clay throughout the whole of 2013. She won at Toronto, the US Open, Beijing and the WTA Championships. It was a phenomenal season. The year 2013 would be the most successful of her career so far with eleven titles won, including two at Grand Slam level. Over the last year and a half she had won one hundred and fourteen matches and suffered just five defeats – a winning ratio of ninety-six per cent. She had become the oldest world number one in history and was still there.

As she had done the previous year, Serena suffered another injury in Australia in 2014 when her back locked up. At Dubai she seemed to lose all her energy. She still won the tournaments in both Miami and Rome despite suffering another injury in Madrid. She eventually suffered an early defeat at Roland-Garros. She seemed to be paying the price for the year and a half of insane success which she had lived through with such intensity.

At Wimbledon she was at her lowest ebb mentally. It was as if she was empty. She had no strength left, but she refused to pull out of the tournament. She was not going to slip away quietly. That's not the way she does things. But she had become less efficient in her matches and had started again to be dominated in the rallies.

"The best way to predict the future is to create it."
Abraham Lincoln

After the traumatising experience of Wimbledon, we needed to sit down, talk and work out how to climb back up the mountain.

Once again I was staggered by her ability to react. We decided to start again from scratch and to rebuild again the fundamentals of her game. She redoubled her efforts in practice. The American swing that followed was a great success. She won in Stanford, Cincinnati and then the US Open, where she won the title without losing a single set. Serena was back on top of the world. By winning her 18th Grand Slam title, she equalled the records of Martina Navratilova and Chris Evert.

In October she won the WTA Championships again. She ended the season on top of the world rankings for the second year in a row, which she had never done before.

11
The 2015 Australian Open

*"Champions live in a state of
permanent dissatisfaction."*

As long as Serena kept her motivation, her desire to play and to continue breaking records, I would stay by her side. What could be more motivating for a coach who is wedded to his profession and who wants to play a part in writing the sport's history than to accompany a great champion as she attempts to realise her ambitions?

I am a relentless worker and unhealthily ambitious. Like a champion, I am eternally dissatisfied. Whenever I reach a target, I am immediately looking to the next one. I pursue many goals at the same time.

Serena had set herself a new challenge, that of beating the record number of Grand Slam titles. Was it what she wanted or what I wanted? I had to be clear about that. I had to assure myself that she wanted it from deep within her. That would be essential if she was to achieve such an enormous task. And if it was the case, the emergence of new talent from all corners of the world in the constantly changing landscape of women's tennis would mean that Serena would have to continue to develop her game.

She is a true chameleon, someone who bridges the generations by managing to remain competitive at the highest level, even at the age of thirty-three. I worked on a new development plan for her. If she was to continue to reign, she would need to move forward constantly. Tennis is a sport in permanent evolution. Every player must be constantly evolving too.

There are two options in this sport: you either progress or you are condemned to go backwards, because others will move past you.

December 2014, Miami,
pre–season preparations for 2015
Sat in the drawing room of Serena's house at Palm Beach Gardens, we discussed our work objectives for the year ahead. We were completely in agreement about the skills that she needed to develop and the areas on which we needed to focus and concentrate our efforts.

We worked hard. I was totally satisfied with her application. The idea of adding extra dimensions to her game motivated her. Her serve needed particular attention. I suggested a small technical adjustment. For the last eighteen months I hadn't been happy with the rewards she had been reaping from her serve. I was convinced that she had plenty of room for improvement in terms of effectiveness.

On 2 January we flew to Perth in Australia to play in the Hopman Cup. I was not satisfied with her results in this competition. She lacked desire and energy. She suffered from a lack of motivation. We had a forthright discussion after she did not really try during a 6-2, 6-2 defeat by young Eugenie Bouchard.

Such behaviour is very unlike Serena, which was why I was concerned about it. I needed to understand what she was feeling inside in order to help her react. The Australian Open was looming very quickly on the horizon. From now onwards, everything we did had to be geared towards doing well in that tournament.

Our preparations for the Grand Slam tournament went very well. The aim was to prepare Serena in such a way that she got progressively stronger from the first week onwards so that she was playing her best tennis in the second week.

When I saw her draw, I concluded that it was not favourable. However, I knew deep down that the outcome depended only on Serena. She would have to dig into her own resources earlier than I had expected, that was all. I knew that if you have pretensions to win Grand Slam titles you need to be capable of beating every player in the draw.

After beating Alison van Uytvanck in the first round, Serena beat Russia's Vera Zvonareva, a former world No. 2, 7-5, 6-0. When she came off the court she was not happy with her game. She said to me: "I want to go back out there and practise straight away. I played really badly." That attitude pleased me. I knew her motivation was back at its highest level. When we went back out, Zvonareva was already on an adjoining court. She had also decided to go back to work immediately because she was not happy with the match she had played. It was a good lesson in professionalism and determination.

In the third and fourth rounds, Serena faced two promising young players: Elina Svitolina, who is a member of my academy, and the celebrated Garbine Muguruza, who had humiliated Serena 6-2, 6-2 in the second round at Roland-Garros. Without playing her best tennis, but by relying on the quality of her first serve and her fighting powers, Serena managed to beat both of these young hopefuls in three sets.

Serena then hit 13 aces in beating Dominika Cibulkova, who had been the runner–up in 2014, and overcame the youngster Madison Keys in the semi-finals. Keys had beaten Venus in the quarter-finals, hitting 17 aces in the process. In one of the best finals in recent years Serena beat Maria Sharapova for the 16th time in a row, winning 6-3, 7-6. Serena hit 18 aces in the match, which was an impressive tally.

By winning this Australian Open Serena had won her 19th Grand Slam title. That took her ahead of Chris Evert and Martina Navratilova and put her three behind Steffi Graf, who holds the record in the Open era. I knew it would not be the last time that Serena amazed me.

12
Observations on French tennis

"Men have great pretension and small plans."
                                                    Vauvenargues

I love my country deeply. During the ten years in which my job as a coach has taken me around the world all year long, I have realised even more how privileged I have been, in so many respects, to be French and to live in what I consider to be one of the finest countries in the world. A nomad for most of the year, I appreciate even more every moment that I spend in the country of my birth. Beyond this, I cherish French culture – my culture – as one of the richest and most passionate in the whole world.

On the other hand I often deplore certain ways of thinking and I like to believe that we are in the process of changing them.

I often ask myself: what is the difference between our French players and the Federers, Nadals, Murrays and Djokovics – and the likes of

Wawrinka, Cilic and Del Potro, who have each won Grand Slam titles? It's obviously not a question of talent, nor of natural physical qualities. From this point of view the French players have nothing to be envious about with regard to anyone else.

> *"Haters will see you walk on water*
> *and say it's because you can't swim."*
>
> anonymous

What I have to say about this is not to accuse any individuals but an attempt to understand the situation, so that we can move forward and so that future generations can benefit from these reflections. I am not condemning anyone, not least because I am fundamentally convinced that every individual has the capacity to evolve. My purpose is to be constructive about this; the attacks that I have been subjected to in the press after expressing my opinions on this subject show that certain people feel threatened whenever they are called into question. There is only one way to go forward, to grow, to stop making the same mistakes. Moreover, these "reactions" are evidence of the climate which prevails in our country. We will not win if we are divided. We must be united.

What I have to say may threaten certain individual interests, but we need to see beyond that. We have everything that we need to be successful at the highest level provided we look ourselves in the face and provided we are able to call ourselves into question. How we are viewed from outside is always interesting and should be taken into account…

In France we suffer from a lack of ambition. People point at those who succeed. To be appreciated it is better to be average and not make any noise. The thinking that prevails is this: "Let's be happy and keep our heads below the parapet." Someone like Teddy Riner, for example, dares to express these values. Why in France do we castigate those who believe in themselves? Let's not confuse self-confidence with self-importance, ambition and opportunism. Rather than develop a form of jealousy in the face of those who are successful and single them out for criticism, let us be inspired by them. This state of mind affects every stratum of our society, including, unfortunately, top-level sport. It is the reason why those of us in charge at the highest level – the coaches, the tennis federation, the leagues, private organisations – should promote those values that have the best chance of producing champions. All young people are influenced by the environment in which they develop. It's our job to create an atmosphere which pulls players up to the top.

Let's put an emphasis on values such as work, investment in our business, ambition rather than talent and contentment. You never build anything big without work, self-sacrifice and suffering. Let's push to the front those who give themselves the means to realise their ambitions, let's hold them up as examples, let's be proud of our successes and of those who fly the French flag on high. That is the best message we can send to the younger generations.

13
What am I chasing?

"We have two lives.
The second begins when we realize we have only one."
Confucius

Being a coach is the job of my life. Beyond this intense and demanding activity, I am involved in several other areas.

I remain passionate about my adventure with the Mouratoglou Tennis Academy so long as we continue to achieve results at international level, we put into practice the coaching methods which I have developed by working for twenty years with the best juniors and professional players and we enable every youngster to blossom and to succeed in a programme which brings together education and top-level sport. I derive even greater pleasure from the fact that we have moved to Sophia-Antipolis in the south of France, where we are building what will be the best and most modern training establishment in Europe.

I created my Champ'Seed foundation in December 2014 in order to support the best young tennis talent from around the world. My aim with this project is to help determined and talented youngsters who are lacking only in the means to exploit their potential in our sport.

I am also busy with my work as a television consultant. I am working on my own programme (*The Coach*) which will see light of day on Eurosport international at Roland-Garros 2015 and will be broadcast every day in 54 countries.

As I love coaching and sharing, I also help businesses which provide group or individual training programmes for managers.

What am I chasing? A certain concept of happiness, no doubt about that. I want to exploit every area of my potential. I love adventures. I need challenges.

In pushing myself to the maximum of my potential, I feel that I am respecting myself. I will not accept the idea that I might one day regret that I did not push myself as far as I could. Our time on this Earth is short. I want my time to be intense, rich in emotion, powerful. I want to be proud of what I have accomplished.

I am convinced that all of us have a potential which is much greater than we imagine. We have infinite possibilities. What gives me a great desire to get up in the morning is the prospect of exploring new areas, seeing plans through, putting myself in danger, going places where I am not expected to go.

My job consists of enabling my students to go beyond their limits in order to make their dreams possible. In order to achieve that I need to make them demand more of themselves, to teach them to be more precise in their work and to improve the quality of their concentration.

Finally, my happiness and my success are tied up with each other. When I think back to that first Wimbledon final that Serena and I won together, her expression remains forever engraved on my memory. I see again her joy and this immense happiness which made her so radiant. I remember her embrace when she climbed up into the stands to take me in her arms and share that magical moment with me. Those moments justify all the sacrifices and the thousands of hours of work and suffering.

14
What they say about me

"I'm not conceited.
I just have enormous confidence in myself."
Novak Djokovic

Jérémy Chardy,
number 29 in the ATP rankings

"Meeting Patrick saved me. We met when I was going through the most difficult period of my career. I was at my lowest point, both in my mind and in my game. He took me under his wing as if I was his own child. He supported me and enabled me to get my head out of the sand."

"Since first meeting up with him, my relationship with tennis has totally changed, because he helped me to develop my love of the game. Through all these years that I have spent at his academy, he has helped me to develop both as a player and as a man."

"I will never be able to thank him enough for

what he has done for me."

"Like other players, I was lucky enough that my path crossed with his. He's a great coach and a formidable human being."

"He has become a very dear friend in whom I have total confidence."

Anastasia Pavlyuchenkova, number 17 in the WTA rankings

"Patrick has an enormous number of qualities, but one of the greatest is his result–based culture. He has always been completely sure of what he wants out of life. He has set his targets and reached them."

Yanina Wickmayer, number 11 in the WTA rankings and semi–finalist at the 2009 US Open

"Patrick is the best coach I have worked with. Not just because he knows this sport better than anyone, but also because he knows me as a person.

He's a great man who has been a true inspiration for me over the years."

Martina Hingis, former world number one, winner of five Grand Slam tournaments

"I was lucky to work alongside Patrick at his academy for a year and a half. Being able to appreciate the energy and passion he showed for the sport was a great experience. If tennis was available on the menu, he would order it for breakfast, for lunch and even for dinner! The only person I have known who has the same enthusiasm for this sport is my mother…"

"Sometimes when the day was over and we had finished the work with the players, we stayed on the court and exchanged shots with each other from the baseline. We were like two raging lunatics who could never be satisfied. We loved challenging each other and putting into practice what we had coached our players to do. There was no better adrenaline with which to feed our love of the sport than to hit a winning backhand down the line – and he always gave me back my own medicine… I love remembering the joy that we had together on the court!"

"Watching him work with his students, I appreciated that he always gave one hundred and twenty per cent. The players had total respect for him and trusted him. That is indispensable for anyone wanting to improve their game and it was something that he always managed to achieve."

"He was always able to read their minds and to convince them that he was right and that they had to adopt such or such a strategy. He prepares his players for matches perfectly; it is then their job to carry out his plans."

"His work with Serena Williams is an excellent example of what he is capable of doing. Before they got together, she had stopped winning. He put her back on her feet, gave her renewed motivation and shared his love of the game with her."

"From that day onwards she became almost unbeatable. It's for all those reasons that I call Patrick Mouratoglou the 'Mentalist'."

"From a friend of the game."